CHARISMATIC VIOLENCE

(BASED ON A TRUE STORY)

CHARISMATIC VIOLENCE
(BASED ON A TRUE STORY)

Yvonne Swain

HZZ Grace Book Publishing
Cedar Park, TX

CHARISMATIC VIOLENCE
Published by:
HZZ GRACE Book Publishing
Cedar Park, Texas

Yvonne Swain, Publisher & Editorial Director
QualityPress.info, Book Packager

ALL RIGHTS RESERVED

No part of this book may be reproduced or transmitted in any form or by any means – electronic or mechanical, including photocopying, recording or by any information storage and retrieved system without written permission from the authors, except for the inclusion of brief quotations in a review.

HZZ Grace Books are available at special discounts for bulk purchases, sales promotions, fund raising or educational purposes.

© Copyright 2020 by Yvonne Swain
ISBN #:978-1-0878-8081-5
Library of Congress Control Number: 2020908254

DEDICATION

This book is Dedicated to my Mother.
I believe it is time to tell your story.
I want you to know that when it was all
said and done. I loved you Mommy.
No matter what.

Charismatic Violence

ACKNOWLEDGEMENTS

I want to thank my Daughters Janai, Symone and Jordin. The beats of my heart. My three miracle babies whom my Mother adored. Thank you for being the amazing encouraging Queens that you are. I am so proud of the Women you have become, and I thank you for pushing me to "finish the book Mommy". I love you. To Paityn, Cannon and Baby J, Grandma is inspired by you.

I want to thank my Husband Clarence for imparting in me a confidence I have never had. With an unselfish love that understood and accepted me with all the baggage I carried. It was you who said, "I'm not going anywhere, finish your book." It was your love that stood strong when I would cry. You are my protector, my Hero. It was your arms that held me through the tears of my memories.

I want to thank my Brothers Charles, Brian and Chuckie and my Sisters Shawn and Melodie. We made it. We did it! We broke the curse. We prayed over our children, then watched God show up and show out. They said our children weren't going to be anything. They said our children weren't going to accomplish anything, but we proved them all wrong! We prayed and God stayed. I love you five with all of my heart and there is nothing that will ever keep me from loving you unconditionally. All things aside we survived!

To my Sister in Law I say thank you Diane for pushing through and praying for us and giving us the love that a Sister in Law should and would give.

To the Wilsons, I say thank you for never giving up on us, the children. For always extending encouraging words and teaching us the value of hard work. Most of all, thank you for holding on to us for dear life. Refusing to let us fall away from you and always reminding us, all six, that we were loved. Stephanie Robin and Sandy I could not have completed this without you. The Wilsons for wondering, "where are they?" and then searching for us and finding us.

To the Yorks, I say thank you to those of you who stood in the gap. Who fought against the violence and who lived and survived. I remember... my Cousin Dennis who would

Acknowledgements

randomly show up to check on me and protected me whenever he could. Love you Cousin Dennis Lee Alfred.

In tears, I write thank you to my closest friends of 39 years. Crystal, Sondra and Traci, I thank you for living through this with me. For we shared similar households and we comforted each other at different times. Nothing will come between friends who carried and loved each other through pain. I thank you for all the times you told me to "write the book, finish your book or put what you feel in your book". I love you, my hearts.

To my Stepmom Mildean and my Father. I love you and although this may touch home I appreciate your support in allowing me to heal by telling my truth. Your encouragement and love have given me the strength to push out this project and to ...finally...heal.

To Tony and Yvonne Rose and Amber Books, this vision, this healing could not have happened without the foresight and guidance brought by you. I am forever grateful for you. Thank you for encouraging me to tell my story. Love you guys at Amber Books and the professionalism you give throughout the process.

Charismatic Violence

And finally, to my Aunt Shirley and my Aunt Katherine, this is for Your Sister to whom you issued unconditional love. I love you both so much. Thank you for coming whenever and every time Momma called. Thank you for walking into situations that could have cost you your lives. Thank you for all of the times, YOU saved my Mother's life and the lives of her Children.

CONTENTS

Dedication	v
Acknowledgements	vii
Contents	xi
Prologue	xv
Foreword	xvii
The Audition	1
Fire Away	6
Joey's Mom	9
Lil Michael	16
Cousin Mike	19
Me and Sidney	24
Mom Moaning on the Floor	31
Aunt Deena's Story	33
Demon Seeds	37
Mom on Drugs	55
Aunt Breanna	58
Mentally Tired	69
Grocery Store Reality	70
Annette	72

Sexual Learning	79
Babysitting and Haircare	84
Evil Education	91
Getting High	96
Smokey Robinson	101
California	108
Something Weird	111
Foster Care	113
The Story	125
Return to the War Zone	128
Surprise Siblings	133
Being Angry	137
For Whatever Reason	141
Fighting	145
New Attitude	153
School Days	171
South High School	174
Mrs. Bette cox	178
Reggie	183
The Bus	188
Quiet Interrupted	193
Why whisper?	197
Uncle Brothers	201
On Killing Your Cousin	210
On Swinging	213

Contents

Leave My Husband Alone 217
Other 222
A Biting Auntie 225
The Concert 227
Fighting My Dad about College 232
Fort Morgan 239
Deal With the Devil 252
Hotel Motel 260
So It Is That I Am 264
Epilogue 269
About the Author 275

Charismatic Violence

PROLOGUE

The names have been changed
The history is stained with the blood of the pain
The names have been changed
The history rains down on secrets for others to gain
The names have been changed
But you know who you are in the still of the hurt
The names have been changed
And you know that with lies you covered your dirt
The names have been changed
To protect the babies whose drama on them you did pile
The names have been changed
And we know your names as we look in the
eyes of your Child.

Charismatic Violence

FOREWORD

"You were a mistake." For as long as I can remember my Mother would say that to me. I did not realize until I was 55 that I had spent my life making sure that I was as perfect as possible. Trying to make sure that I did not make mistakes, or if I did, doing my best to fix them immediately. The definition of mistake on dictionary.com is an error in action, calculation, opinion or judgement caused by poor reasoning, carelessness, insufficient knowledge, etc.

According to my Mother, I was not planned and was the cause of my Father marrying her. Not a wedding, but a justice of the peace ceremony with no attendees with the exception of my Mother's parents. My Grandma telling my Mother that she "had better figure out a way to stay with this man, no matter what. You are going to have a child with this man, and you are not going to be able to do it without him."

My Mom said she tried not to believe anything my Grandmother said because she had grown up as "nobody's favorite." Grandma had called me a mistake, as well, before I was born but never to my face.

My Father would call me "not planned" more than the word mistake. My Mother said that while I was in her stomach she felt beautiful. She said her hair grew like the true Indian Woman she believed was in her soul. She said she would read out loud and listen to music while I was in her belly and do her best to sing.

She said she ate lots of potatoes, (I love potatoes), while she was pregnant with me and craved beef everything. She said that she knew it was a girl because she dreamed of pink and she was definitely "not" going to name me "Fleta" even though my Grandma wanted her too. She said that even though I was a "mistake" she was not going to make the mistake of giving me a name that would be made fun of. She said that French was her favorite language, so she decided to name me Yvonne Michelle. She said there would be no mistake in that.

She said she felt amazing being pregnant and that the life inside her was both amazing and challenging at the same time. She was spoiled by my Dad during this time and she could not wait until I was born so we could all become a family.

Foreword

When I was born, My Mother said My Father went out and bought dresses to match his suits. Whenever we would go visit family, my Father would tell my Mother to put me in the same color he was wearing. She said that she was a little jealous at times but could see he truly loved his Daughter.

One day when I was six months old my Mother said she had neglected to put me in the same color as my Dad. When he asked her why she didn't do it she said she was tired, and it really didn't matter. She said he hit her with me in her arms and knocked her in the wall. She said to protect me she turned her shoulder into the wall, and it dislocated. My Father yanked her up and told her to do what he said and then he kicked her in the back.

I was still on the floor crying, but he picked me up and hugged me until I stopped crying. She found an outfit and put it on me.

She went into the room to get dressed and heard the car door slam. My Father had put me in his lap with the seat belt and was pulling out of the yard. She ran through the yard after us through stickers and whatever only for him to yell, "You stay your ass here! This is time for me and my Daughter!"

Charismatic Violence

He came home late into the night with no explanation and would torture her this way for months. It was after that first hit that he would beat her at least once a week. She told me, "I was so confused, I didn't know what had happened or what was going on."

I have not been able to figure out why God allowed my Mother to go through so much pain. I suppose He knew that she would sustain, nonetheless......all the way to the end of her life.

This book speaks to some of those pains and the way it affected not only my Mother but the minds of her children.

This book is not for the purpose of pointing fingers. This book is simply from the perspective of a child with a child's thoughts and a scared mind.

This book is based on a true story, although names have been changed to protect the innocent. Parts of the book are fictional, but most of it is not.

The devil does not want this book to come to fruition. It is because there is a blessing somewhere at the end of this terror, an end to the pain in this story. There is an elephant in the room, a huge one. One that will release the pain and hurt of all in my family and will finally tell the truth.

THE AUDITION

In this story my dad plays the devil. He had auditioned and won. He had wanted to play the part of demon, of devil and he had won a starring role. My Father had been able to, during my time growing up, show his children what kind of devil he could be. He was a man who had internal pain and wanted to demonstrate the severity of this pain to his family.

We were terrified of him. We were only at peace when he was at work, out partying or missing. We prayed that he would die sometimes. We prayed that he would find another woman and never come back. We prayed that he would decide to just leave us and travel somewhere, anywhere! We prayed and prayed but didn't understand why God seemed to ignore us. We weren't to understand until later that this was to be our ministry.

On most days, when my Father would get angry his processed conk would begin to unravel; but it seemed like his hair would only stick up in two places like horns. We began to believe that truly when he was gearing up to beat my Mom, the devil or a demon was inside his body.

It would always be something miniscule like a pot not being clean enough or a dirty glass. He would start by pointing out the error and then yelling about it. His voice would get louder and louder and then he would throw something or break things. He always started with things. Then he would start yelling at US. At first, my Mom would stay quiet; but if he made his way toward us as if to hurt us she would say something to draw his attention back to her. She knew what it meant, and he would make her pay for it. He would turn his attention immediately to her, walk up to her, yell in her face; and then when she didn't expect it, he would hit her.

Generally, the first blow would land her across the room or up in the air. He hit her with power, and he hit her like a man. She was given no mercy. Blow after blow, scream after scream. Wherever we were,, he would instruct us not to move. I always wondered why he wouldn't let us go to our room. Why did we have to witness such craziness?

I realized later that he was actually scared. He was scared that we might just go crazy like him. That we might just go into a room and get a bat and hit him in the back of

The Audition

the head. He was scared that we might grab a knife from the kitchen and stab him in the middle of his back or in the back of his head. What he didn't know was that at one time we were planning to kill him. What stopped us? My Great Grandmother.

We screwed up and told her about our plan and she told us that God would not like that and that if we had to look at Jesus we would never want to have to tell Jesus that we had killed our Father. She told us to pray and that God would take care of it. We did, but it seemed like it was taking forever. In the meantime, the habitual evil surfaced at least five days per week.

I watched the red splatter the pavement. It was dark red and looked like someone was taking a paint brush to decorate the hard grey of the pavement. Every five seconds...splat, splat, splat!

My Mother was on her knees in broad daylight. I could see her brunette wig sway to the side as my Dad punched her in the face. Splat! People from the apartment complex were watching from their windows. Splat! Nobody would help her. Splat! I was a thirteen-year-old girl...standing in the window...urinating on myself...scared to go to the bathroom...scared to move from the window for fear he might see me and come after me...splat!

The neighbors would often gasp or say "damn" when they saw my Dad hit my Mother. They would not help her because my Dad was so nice to them. He was an attractive man, charming, built, about 5'6 and every so often he would Billy Dee Williams his black hair. Meaning he would straight perm his hair so it would lay slick on his head. When he began to process his hair, we knew he was probably cheating on my Mother with another woman.

On most occasions my Father would beat up my Mother and leave her laying in whatever room of the house, bleeding. Once he left I would come out of my room and clean up both her and the room. I would get a washcloth and fill up a wash bowl with cool water. I would wet and wring out the cloth and begin to clean my Mother's face and body. I almost threw up sometimes when the water in the bowl changed from clear to red. I could smell her blood and her sweat and see pieces of her skin on the washcloth. She would whimper and mumble things. As a first grader I would listen to what she said and internalize her pain...but by high school I learned to tune it out.

The Audition

I knew the process, get the bowl, clean her up, help her up, put her in bed, sit by her side until she slept, get back up, get the red bucket from under the sink, warm soapy water, wipe up blood from the floor, wipe up blood and skin from the wall, the chair, the table or whatever room he had finalized his beating of her. Clorox to get rid of the smell and then...throw up.

FIRE AWAY

My very first memory was standing behind my Mother, holding onto her right leg. She was trembling. I could see my Father standing across from us in his white T-shirt... He had his hair processed back, styled like the young Elvis. I knew he was my Daddy. I did not know why he hurt my Mommy, but I know that whenever we left the house he would make my Mommy dress me in the same color he was wearing. If he was wearing blue, then I was to wear blue. If he was wearing red, then I was to wear red. We would hang out together and get ice cream. We would go visit family and I always loved seeing my cousins. My Father worked out, so he was always built up nice and the women loved him because he was handsome, and he was the lead singer of the band. He was no doubt charismatic and charming.

I did not know it, but my Mother says I was two or three at the time and she didn't think I "remembered that". I heard something very loud and then I couldn't hear anything other than a ringing in my ear.

I remember dropping whatever it was I was holding and grabbing my ears. My Father was standing across from my Mother about 5 feet or so. He had on a white t-shirt and these red velvety pants.

After the sound, I looked up at my Dad and his eyes were like quarters. His white t-shirt began to change color. Red raced from his right shoulder and took over the white. It was as if someone was pouring red paint down his right shoulder.

My Mother dropped the gun and started to scream. My Father ran to her and picked her up from the floor. She was crying and saying she was sorry. He was consoling her telling her that he was okay. Her face was full of blood and he was wiping it off with a paper towel. I was standing against the wall, scared, wondering what was going on. The blood continued to run down her face from her forehead.

He begged, "Tell them you fell on your face in the kitchen, ok? Tell them that we were talking about how to use the gun and that's when you fell on your face and accidentally shot me, ok?" She was nodding. "We don't want you to go to jail, because then you will never see your babies again. Do you want that?"

My Mother was weeping hard. Her blood was dripping on the floor. He moved her to the sink. He took the dishcloth and wiped her face again. He buckled, "We have to go now, I'm starting to get weak." They stumbled out of the front door. I heard the car door and pulled a chair up to the sink. I climbed up just in time to see them drive away from the kitchen window. I closed the door and looked at the red stuff on the floor. I put my finger in it and drew a smiley face.

I looked over and saw my dolly. There was blood on her face and on her dress. I picked up Mrs. Beasley and went to my room, which was actually an open back porch. I lay down in the bed with Mrs. Beasley and watched the scary trees blow in the wind. They were scratching the windows looking like scary creatures outside. The trees always tried to get me at night, but my great grandma had told me God wouldn't let them in, but I was still scared.

They kept scratching, louder and louder....especially since they knew Mommy and Daddy were leaving me by myself, more and more.

JOEY'S MOM

Joey was my best friend. We lived right off Eighth Street, together on Troy. We talked about how we were going to be big kids going to kindergarten and then we would get to stay up past our eight o'clock bedtime. Joey was Spanish and he would speak a different language, sometimes with his mom and sometimes they would teach me. Joey would say, "Bueno Evon" and I would say "Bueno Jose."

Joey was skinny like me and his hair was cut like one of the Beatle's. We both liked the Beatles and would sometimes dance in Joey's living room to different songs by the Beatles when Joey's mom would play their music.

Joey's Mom always put Joey in shirts with stripes going across them. Joey liked them because he said the shirts made his chest look big like his Padre's. I thought so. She mostly put Joey in Jeans and the coolest new athletic shoes. Joeys stripes were mostly green and blue, but sometimes red and blue or blue and white. I always looked outside to see what he was wearing and then I would try to wear the same color.

This particular day I looked outside and saw Joey wearing green and blue. I went to my closet and found the dress my Nanna had given me which was plaid dark blue and green with a sailor collar. I was happy because I would match Joey.

When I went outside Joey's mom said 'Oh Miha….you look so pretty!" I smiled and said, "Grashas." She giggled and went back into her house. Joey and I jumped right into the dirt and began to make mud pies and dirt buildings and all the things that 4-year-olds do. When it started to get dark Joey's Mom said, "Joey come in…it's time to eat dinner." He jumped up and waved goodbye… "I heard her say "Oh miho you are so filthy…you need a bath."

I picked myself up and went into the house and closed the door. I was filthy too, but it was about "that" time. When I went into the back-porch room my little brother was now awake. He smiled at me and started to clap his hands. PEW!!! He smelled really bad…but I knew how to change him because Mommy taught me how. I went and got a washcloth, a diaper and some powder. I laid a towel under him and lay him down. He was still laughing. I took off his diaper and started to wipe with tissue. I flushed them down the toilet as I wiped him off. Once I cleaned as much as I could I wiped him with a cloth, put baby powder on his privates and then put on a diaper. He sat up and said, "Baba?" I said, "Yes, my little brother and I started to sing." I sang so he knew I wasn't far, and I filled up his bottle with milk. I also took out a piece of bread and started to roll little balls out of it. I saw Mommy do this sometimes when she would feed him. I would make up songs and sing to him while I fed him the bread and when he wanted to drink he would pick up his bottle. He was my baby brother and I loved him, and I had to take care of him because I had asked God for him.

After my Brother ate and drank we played until wee hours of the night. I had to keep him up so I could play outside the next day. In the morning I woke up and looked outside. Hmmm Joey was wearing blue and green again. So, I put on the same dress. I washed my face and went outside to play. My ruffled white panties however were not so white today. Where did Mommy keep the panties?

After the third day of wearing the same dress Joey's Mom said, "Hello Miha. Where is your Madre." I smiled up at her from the ground. "They are at the store." I had told her the same thing yesterday and the day before. "Miha......who is taking care of your little Brother?" "Oh, I am....since I asked God for him." She lifted her hand to her mouth and shrieked then walked very quickly into her house.

An hour later the police were in front of our home. They walked up to me and said, "Hey pretty girl." I said, "Hello." My Great Grandmother had said not to be afraid of the police. She said they were here to help us and the only people afraid of police were the people who were getting in trouble. The officer reached his hand out to help me up out of the dirt. He didn't even care that my hands were dirty. He walked me over to the police car. I pulled away. "What's wrong?" "My little Brother is sleep in the house and I can't leave him." The first officer waived a come here signal to his partner, "Oh ok. Well let's go get him." I let both of the officers in the house and they began to look around. I heard one say, "Hmmm...paraphernalia." The one holding my hand said, "Yep, stems, seeds."

My Brother said a boisterous "HI!" He wasn't afraid of the police either. The first officer looked at the makeshift diaper I had made out of a towel and he smelled it too. "Ohhhh!" He said to his partner and quickly put my Brother back down on the bed. The second officer began to laugh. "I'll be right back", the first officer left the house. The second

Fire Away

officer sat down and began to talk to me. "So, what is your name?" "Yavon!" "Oh, that is a pretty name." I said, "My Mommy gave it to me." "Oh well that was really nice of her." He smiled and bent down on one knee. I noticed he was looking at the walls. "My Daddy has records on the wall because he sings with a group." "Oh, he does?" "Yes." "Wow that makes your Daddy very cool." I looked into his eyes. "Why are your eyes green?" "Because God wanted me to be different." "Oh...well why are my eyes brown?" He looked me in the eyes......"Because God wanted you to be beautiful." I whispered, "Do you pray?" He smiled. "Yes, I do....especially for all the little children because I have children of my own." "Do your children look like me and my Brother or do they look like Joey?" He smiled, "My children have my color eyes and both of them have yellow hair?" "Oh." He went on..."It is really important for you to know that God makes all children beautiful, all colors with different eyes and shapes and colors."

The first cop walked in with diapers and baby powder. He went into the room and brought my brother to the living room. He went to the kitchen and grabbed some paper towel and wet it in the kitchen sink.

When he removed the towel from my brother he winced. He was holding his breath as the second officer began to laugh. "Dude you went and bought diapers?" "Yeah man....I couldn't let him smell like that." I ran to get my Brother's clothes. I heard my Brother cry out. I ran to the living room...."What's wrong with my Brother?"

The first officer was showing the second officer my Brother's behind and back. It was covered with welts. The officer cleaned my Brother very gently. The second officer asked me, "Yavon, do you hit your Brother, so he is good?' I said, "No, my Daddy hits him every time he pees in the bed. I wash the red stuff off his back after Daddy is done." The first officer had finished changing my Brother and putting on his clothes. They were both crying now. I said, "Don't cry, me and my Brother love you for helping us."

They were crying really hard now. I will remember that day forever. The first time I had interacted with white men and white cops. They kept us all day, took us to McDonald's and out to the playground in a nearby park.

At some point that day we were in the police station and I heard the first officer say to the Black Social worker, "We are going to follow you to the home. I just want to make sure these kids land in a good place." The social worker smiled, looking towards me. "I know the perfect place."

Both officers walked up to the foster home door with us while the social worker explained to the woman we were to stay together and provided a summary of our circumstances. The Officers had made sure we weren't separated and told us they would come and check on us, and they would. The last time I saw the officer he had my Father's shirt in his hand. He said, "If you hurt those kids again, I'll kill you."

LIL MICHAEL

Joey would be my first crush, but "I" was Lil Michael's.

My Father tells a story of a little boy who used to bring me candy when I was about four. He said that the little boy's name was Michael. Apparently, Michael would come to the front step of the projects we lived in and would slide up next to me. Michael always had candy and my Father said he always wondered where Michael had scored the candy from every day.

Michael would hand me the candy and then try to kiss me on the cheek. Father said I would take the candy and put it in my mouth and then from nowhere I wielded a stick. I would take the stick and hit Michael in the head until he would run away crying.

My Father said that he tried to hide the stick from me once and somehow after I ate the candy I still ended up with a stick in my hand to beat Michael. My Father said, 'Where

Lil Michael

did she get that stick??!!" Michael, again, ran away holding his head and crying.

My Father said that one day he went outside and picked up what he thought were all the sticks in the yard. He was trying to help Michael out. Michael kept coming back, no matter how many times I hit him; so, my Father figured he would try to make the environment less hostile. He was sure that now when Michael came over he would not be abused. So, the next morning my Father saw me come out and sit on the front steps of the apartment, as usual. He watched me through the screen, and not long after I was seated, Lil Michael came over and sat down next to me. My Father said he put his head down and lifted his hand up to show me he had candy in it. I took the candy, unwrapped it and put it in my mouth. My Father said, to his disbelief, I lifted my left hand in the air and in it was a stick. My Father said he muttered out loud...."How the hell?!!" I went to whacking this little boy in the head and of course he ran off.

My Dad always laughs when he tells that story and I only wish I knew who Michael was so I could tell him I am so sorry. I wanted to tell him I was sorry because children learn what they live. Poor Michael had obviously seen unconditional love and I had seen taking and violence. What was so funny about that? What little Michael did not know was that he was suffering from the things that were being done to me by Cousin Mike.

COUSIN MIKE

I was five and the school district said my birthday was in October so I would have to wait another year to go to school. I remember crying and my Mother said, "It's ok, Yvonne, you are just going to be automatically smarter than the other kids when you start school." I believed her.

In the meantime, I would be staying with Cousin Mike. He could cook and clean and he was handsome......younger than my Mom, but her favorite cousin. He had long eyelashes and pretty teeth and folks always said he had a good grade of hair and that it lay pretty on his forehead.

I liked him, too. He would take me to the 7 Eleven on Eighth Street and buy me candy. He would talk to me about pretty things like butterflies and ladybugs and told me that even though other people in the family thought I looked like a boy......he thought I was pretty. I told him that Mommy and Aunt Ardra said he was handsome. He said, "Really?" I said, "Yep, and they said you could have any girl you want cuz you look like Billy Dee." "Really?"......he smiled down at me. "Well what do you think?" I said, "I think you are handsome too! But I don't know who Billy Dee is...is he our cousin?" Mike laughed a deep and silky laugh. Initially I thought he was good, and he made me feel like the prettiest girl in the world.

Mom was now working days where she used to work nights and would sleep during the day, while Cousin Mike kept an eye on me. When she went to days, she told Mike my nap schedule and how to take care of my baby brother. I watched Mike take care of my Brother and he did a good job. He changed him and washed him and fed him. I loved my little Brother more than anything in the world and I was happy to see my little Brother laughing and cooing. Mike sang my little brother to sleep and then said, "OK little girl....it is time for you to come and be with me." I always shut my eyes tightly when he was doing his touching. He had even begun to lay on me with his clothes off but was careful.

"Ow", I said. "It's okay, Cousin Mike really loves you and isn't trying to hurt you." I trusted his milky voice. "I have to check me too." He stood up and pulled down his pants and began to rub himself.

He rubbed me and himself until he made a low growl. The growl scared me, and I began to cry. "He ran out of the

Cousin Mike

room and came back with a warm towel and clean panties. "Don't cry....it is something I have to do to make sure we are both ok...but don't tell your Mom because then she will die, and you will never see her again."

"Okay", I said as he cleaned me up. He put fresh panties on me and said, "Now go to sleep and when you wake up Cousin Mike will take you to the store." I went to sleep and when I woke up everything was butterflies and ladybugs again.

As the weeks wore on, Cousin Mike became rougher and rougher and didn't care if I cried. I would squeeze my legs together and shut my eyes tightly when he was doing his touching. He had even begun to lay on me with his clothes off but was careful not to penetrate. I hated 7-Eleven now and he stopped talking while we walked to the store.

One day after another rough session with Cousin Mike I asked God to "please make it stop. God it really hurts me and no one else can see but you see everything. Please I did not like him on me but when my Mom took me to my Grandma's house they would scowl or roll their eyes. So, my Mom did not like taking me over there for them to babysit. My Grandmommy couldn't badger her or make her cry when

Mike was watching me. So, I was hurt for at least a year. Every day I prayed that God would make him go away.

One day as I was eating lunch, I heard my great grandmother scream! Oh my God no!!" I ran into the bedroom, "What's wrong Nanna?" "OH baby...I bet it's going to affect her the most......she was so close to him...Okay, I won't say anything to her....I will let you tell her."

Later that afternoon my Mother came to pick me up from Nanna's and she said, "Vonnie, your cousin Mike has gone to heaven." I was mad... Why did God take him to heaven, and he was doing mean stuff to me??!! I just stood there and gave my mom a mean look. "Why MOMMIE!!" "Well honey, because God sometimes takes people before we are ready......" She went on to explain and I was in my own world.

Later that evening, when all the family was over, I was in the doorway eavesdropping on the adults talking about what had happened to Cousin Mike. "Apparently Mike was riding his motorcycle and a truck hit him. His body went into the ravine, but his head was found on the road."

My eyes were big, and I grabbed my mouth to keep from screaming. I jumped down on my knees and said, 'God I did

Cousin Mike

not mean for you to kill him....I just meant for you to take him away!" It was at that time that I began to believe that God means business and that when I prayed to God for something, he would in fact deliver so I had better really need him when I called him.

At Cousin Mike's funeral, my Mother walked me to his casket and expected me to cry. I didn't, but the congregation did....they thought we were so close. I heard my Mom tell people, "She is just in shock....she will cry later". I never cried.

ME AND SIDNEY

Me and Sidney were always together when I spent the weekends with my Nanna. We did everything together and Nanna would let me go play with her often. Sidney "always" had candy and she always shared it with me. I remember my Aunt May asking Sidney where she was getting all the candy, but Sidney always had an answer. "Momma I got it from Chaz." Aunt Mae would not question it….she would just say, "Oh, okay." Sidney would giggle.

One day I asked Sidney where she was getting all the candy and she told me that I could get candy too, but all I had to do was go to the bathroom. I frowned at her, "What?" She grabbed my hand. "Come on cousin.'" She took me to the neighbor's house right in front of her's. I remember the house being pink and very clean inside. There were no pictures on the wall, but there were doilies on tables, lamps and throws over the couch. I remember the throws having deer on them.

Me and Sidney

Sidney told me the guy inside was one of our older cousins and that he was related to us, somehow. He was skinny and started ringing his hands together when we walked in. He was smiling hard at us and he seemed to almost skip as he walked around the house. "Sidney, you brought a friend with you?" "Yes," she said. "And she wants some candy, too." "Oh, how fun. Well, we will make sure that happens."

Sidney winked at me. He was shaking and his eyes were big as quarters. "So, who would like to go first?" Sidney said in her perky voice, "I will, I will!" He motioned toward the bathroom and Sidney walked in. I heard the toilet seat go up and then a brief moment of quiet. I heard the sound of pants unzipping and then Sidney whispering, "Ow, that hurts not so fast, go slow, go slowww, ow." I heard the toilet lid hit the back of the toilet a couple of times and him whispering..."shhhhh, it's ok...." Then, "See, it just takes a minute."

It seemed like forever; but then, I heard the water running and then Sidney came out. The older cousin walked past me smiling and gave Sandy a big glad sandwich bag of candy. All I could remember was wanting my own bag of candy.

He motioned for me to come with him. I got up and followed him into the bathroom. Everything was white and cold, the tile ,the sink and the towels hanging over the rack. He told me to take off my shorts and to try to go to the bathroom. I told him I didn't have to go. He told me to face the back of the toilet and sit with my legs spread open. "Grab the toilet seat."

He lowered his voice and moved closer to me. He pushed my back forward and pulled my back so that my bottom was lifted slightly up. I felt something cold and creamy between my bottom cheeks and I jumped. "No!" He began to massage my bottom. "It's ok...this will just help you boo boo easier, then when you do that I can give you your candy. Don't you want your candy bag?" I nodded my head. He was putting a lot of cream on me now and was using a finger to push a little cream inside me.

I would wince a little when he put his finger a little deeper. "I am going to put a little bigger finger this time, ok?" He went from using his pinky finger to using his pointer finger, or at least that is what he said. "I remember that hurting more and I told him, "NO...I don't want any candy anymore!" He took his finger out and said, 'Its ok, Sidney did it......we just have to add more cream." I felt the cold cream being rubbed on me again. I also heard a fast slapping sound behind me. I felt something much bigger now rubbing in between the cheeks of my behind. It wasn't going in, but it was certainly bigger than a finger. He was moaning.

Then before I could take another breath I felt the head of his penis penetrate my bottom. The pain was unbearable. I screamed and stood up on both feet. He was trying to grab me and push me back down onto the toilet. I was screaming as loud as I could. I want someone, anyone to hear me. "Help Me! Stop it!! Please! Anybody help me!!!" My cousin Sidney was at the door. She was screaming and crying! "Leave my cousin alone! Let her out, or I am going to tell!"

He pushed me to the floor. "Get outta here and don't you tell, or I will kill you and your cousin!" I grabbed my panties and shorts and put them on as fast as I could. I opened the bathroom door and Sidney and I ran out of the house. Sidney told me not to tell or we would not get any candy, but she told me to go back home to Nanna's. I ran home, crying. I did not care about the candy. When I got back to Nanna's I went right into the bathroom. I wanted to get all that cream stuff off of me, but Nanna intercepted. "Girl what's wrong with you? You know better than to run..."

Charismatic Violence

She stopped talking and looked at my face. "What happened?" I started crying and told her everything. For some reason, I knew it would be ok to tell her and so I did. I told her every little detail. She listened and assured me that no harm was going to come to me. She assured me that it was not my fault and that there were people in this world who had problems. She ran a hot bath for me and washed me up. She took my underwear and clothes out of the bathroom and brought in some fresh clothes. She gave me some time alone in the tub.

I heard her pick up the phone, but I could not hear what she said. Oh God, please don't let her have told anyone. They will think I am a bad girl. After my bath I put my clothes on and opened the bathroom door. I could hear my Nanna talking to someone. I walked quietly through the kitchen to the living room and peeked around the corner. I saw my Nanna showing my Uncle Evan my panties. He was calm and then to the right was my Uncle Wade and my Uncle Joe. They were all very quiet. My Uncle Evan saw me. "Hello beautiful". He motioned me into the living room.

My Nanna stepped aside. The all stood in front of me. "You didn't do anything wrong," my Uncle Evan stated in a quiet voice. I looked at each one in the face and they were nodding their heads. "We love you and we promise you will never have to worry about that ever happening again." They asked me to come with them and Nanna and show them the house I was in. I said, "OK".

I was walking up the street with them and when we were halfway there they asked me if I saw the house I was in. I told them "Yes, it's that pink one." My Nanna grabbed my hand and said, "Good girl. Now you and I are going home to make ice cream." We turned in the opposite direction from my uncle's and I realized now that my Nanna kept me talking so I would not look back.

I went back to my Nanna's about a month later and of course went to visit my cousin Sidney. My Nanna walked me there this time. After my Nanna walked away, I asked Sidney if she had gotten any more candy. She said, "No." She said that she thought he had gone away because no one could find him.

She said a window was open though and she had climbed in, but he was never there. "Wanna see?" I followed her to the window, and we climbed in. We were walking all over the house, but the house was not so clean. There was dust and leaves and bugs crawling around. Sidney said she was going to his room to look for candy. I told her to hurry because it was getting dark. I went to the bathroom and slowly opened the door. The red rag he used was still on the floor but some of the tile on the perfect white floor were now broken and some of the white tile on the walls were busted. Where was the mirror? The window was now covered with wood. I took a deep breath and closed the door.

MOM MOANING ON THE FLOOR

When I would return from Nanna's, most assuredly, there would be some sort of drama. Especially, if my Mother had someone else pick us up to bring us home. This time it was my Aunt Deena. Aunt Deena greeted my Great Grandmother with respect and hugs and my Great Grandmother loved her right back. They spoke for a brief moment and my Aunt Deena stated that she had to hurry and get us back to my Mother, as she truly missed us.

She was rushing us along, "Come on, kids let's get our things." We were jumping up and running to get our things. We loved Aunt Deena, she was fun, and she loved us. She always stood up for us and always would fight my Dad on behalf of my Mom. We walked out the door after kissing my Nanna. And just before I got in the car, I heard my Nanna ask my Aunt Deena a question, " How is Fleta?" My Aunt Deena looked at the ground. "She is okay, I guess." My Nanna said, " You have blood on your shirt, I see it through the sweater."

Charismatic Violence

My Aunt Deena kept looking at the ground, "I know". She pulled away from My Nanna and jumped in the car. The drive home was fun. Aunt Deena found games to play while we drove home. Games like find the circle shapes or let me know when you see things or signs that are yellow. Or pick your favorite car. She always kept us busy when we were with her.

We arrived at the house and when we opened the door we saw broken pictures and things thrown all over the place. I smelled "the smell'. The smell of my Dad's sweat and the smell of my Mother's blood and skin. My Mother was in the bed, but she was already cleaned up. My Aunt Deena must have done it and she must have run my Dad out of there.

My Mom was in the bed with both eyes closed from being beaten. Her mouth was enlarged from punches to the face. My Aunt Deena went in the room and closed the door behind her, but I had already seen my Mom. "The kids are here, and they are safe, my heart." I could hear my Mom gurgle something that sounded like thank you. I was sad to clean up all the mess, but I was glad my Aunt Deena was here.

AUNT DEENA'S STORY

My Aunt Deena stood by my Mom through thick and thin. She would fight my Father if she was there to keep him from hitting my Mom. She was the youngest girl in my Father's family, but the roughest. She would yell at my Father and tell him he was wrong, whenever she saw my Mom hurt...and sometimes she too would cry. Often she would come over to the house and try to sit there. It seemed my Father did not want to hit my Mom when my Aunt Deena was there.

Aunt Deena had grown up as the baby of my Father's family. She was a spitfire but kindhearted. She would tell a person exactly how she felt, but always would insist on doing what was right. She had a great Spanish friend named Lisa who was so close to her that they had used each other to learn how to kiss boys. They also encouraged each other to do "other" things with boys, as well. I would listen to them sometimes, but pretended I was playing with dolls.

Whenever they would look over at me I would pretend to be really into my dolls.

Because Aunt Deena was so promiscuous she was to come up pregnant. I heard the adults - my Grandmommy and my Aunt Belinda discussing what to do. Aunt Deena wanted her baby but was told, "Baby you can have a baby later in life. We are not ready for you to have a baby right now. Your sister has already brought shame on this family and we don't need that again."

Grandmommy told Aunt Deena to go with Aunt Belinda and she was going to take care of it. Aunt Deena looked at me. Lisa pulled me close to her side and said, "Aye Mommy I don't think this is going to be good."

Aunt Deena came back in severe pain....she was screaming. She was crying in pain and Grandmommy and Aunt Belinda were putting rags on her head and putting her in an ice tub. She was screaming and bleeding in the tub....they would add more ice she would scream......more blood in the water......finally, after she began to shake uncontrollably they took her to the hospital.

When we arrived there the doctor asked, "WHO DID THIS!" The two women looked at each other and said, "We

Aunt Deena's Story

don't know, she went to someone and didn't tell us nothing"....The doctor scowled, "She could have been killed!" I knew they were lying. I was angry! Aunt Deena was the nice one...she was the kind one. She was the one who stuck up for my Mommy. She was the one who stuck up for us.

A week later when Aunt Deena came home I listened and pretended to play with my dolls as she told the story to Lisa. 'My Aunt Belinda took me to her house, and she told me to go into her room and get a towel. She said she was going to help me get rid of my baby. I went into Aunt Belinda's room and sat on her bed. When she came in the room she had a hanger, but it was untwisted so it was long and straight, so the hook was on the end. I started begging her to let it be and she told me to shut the hell up and lay down on the towel and open my legs. She ripped off my underwear and started shoving her hand up me! It hurt and then she was poking me saying "Be still...I'm tryin' to find the hole!"

She then shoved the hanger up me...It hurt going in and she was cutting me inside just to get up in there and then she stuck it in my stomach cuz I felt it and then I felt a rush of stuff and it was blood and stuff. I was screaming because I was in so much pain and then I saw pieces of stuff coming out. Aunt Belinda was like, "Yeah, that's what I'm talkin' about! Now we getting' somewhere!" She said that and she kept poking and pulling and then I passed out.

When I woke up, she had me in her shower! She was screaming at me telling me, "Wake my ass up!" Lisa was crying, "Oh Mommy, I am so sorry". They were holding each other crying now. I put my Dolly down and went and hugged my Aunt Deena, "I will love you forever, Aunt Deena." We all cried that night.

It wasn't until many years later that I heard Aunt Deena say, "Well something happened to me when I was young and now I can't have children." It was at that very moment that I told myself that I would have them for her. She never asked, but I would have.

DEMON SEEDS

It would not be the last time we would experience the demon seeds. My Father just decided that we would only meet up with them at my Grandmommy's house...which was a mistake.

We would sit on the plastic couch and not move until SHE said so. Any infraction of this rule would result in a beating with an extension cord. Most times she would come into the living room and look at us and say, "hmph". About an hour or two later she would say..."Ok, go put your coats in that back room on your cousin's bed. Don't mess up anything and don't touch anything! There is a ghost back there from some dead white woman, so if you see her don't be scared. Somebody killed her in this house, and we think she is somewhere buried in the yard." The truth of the matter is everyone believed that to be true. The room stayed icy cold and whenever we spent the night we felt like someone was watching, standing over us. There were already demons here and quite frankly the dead ones in this house were nicer than the ones who were alive.

We went back to the plastic couch and sat down. She asked us if we were hungry. My Brother and Sister looked at me to answer. Sometimes she would yell if we said yes; but today I answered for all of us. "Yes ma'am".

She slammed a pillow down on the floor and growled at us. She went into the kitchen and we heard her opening the bread. She had three pieces of bread in her hands and she had put her fingers through the pieces. "Here!" She threw a piece of bread at each of us. We all caught them and then stared at her. "Well eat it!" We began to eat slow with our eyes wide. We didn't dare say anything else. She went in the kitchen and fixed herself some potatoes and onions. She sat at the dining room table and ate, and we made sure to keep our eyes fixed on the television. We were not allowed to sit at her table. She made sure we knew that we were dogs, not worthy of sitting at her table to eat.

After she ate, she would sit down to watch one of her soap operas and often would give us an update of who was doing who. If we were quiet she would fall asleep and then we could play. We knew how to play thumb and hand games quietly so she wouldn't wake up. She would sleep all day for the most part, but she had trained me to wake her up at 4:30 in the afternoon so she could make us "look right" before my Daddy or Mommy came to pick us up.

So, I would tell my Brother and Sister to go to the bathroom before she woke up. They would go quietly and then I would go last and flush the toilet so that if she woke up it would be right at 4:30 and she could not do anything.

When I woke her up at 4:30, she would hustle all three of us to the bathroom. She would wash our faces and hands and then lotion them with baby lotion. She would hum while she was cleaning our faces and hands. She would make us get our coats and hold them in our laps until our Daddy came to pick us up. When he walked in, he would hug us and say how good we smelled and that he was so glad Grandmommy was watching us. She would hug him and ask him about work and then give him a hoghead cheese or pork chop sandwich. There was always a negative statement about my Mom, "Well I cook for you because I know that rail of a wife of yours does not know how to cook." My Daddy would hug her and give her a kiss on the cheek and then we would leave.

If my Mother came to pick us up, the scene was altogether different. When my Mom walked in the door we would smile. We loved our Mother! She always looked beautiful, even with the cuts and bruises; but she knew how to cover them up. My Grandmother would say, "I cleaned up your kids, why are they always so dirty?" That was not true, my Mother kept us clean and our clothes pressed. My Dad would not let her buy us new ones, mostly Goodwill; but Momma made it work. Most times he took her money out of her purse, anyway.

My Grandmommy would try to goat my Mother into saying something to her so she could tell my Father. She wanted my Mother to get beaten. My Mother was wise to the game, so she would just remain silent.

This day they mentally abused my Mother. They belittled her in one way or another and subsequent to her leaving my Grandmother made a ritual out of not feeding us.

My parents...mostly my Father...were glad that I was at my Grandmommy's. He thought we were in a loving place, a place where HE was pampered. A place where HE was adored and doted on. He thought that the love he received from his Mother was the same love she was giving us. He was wrong.

What he did not realize was that his Mother hated our Mother. His Mother was jealous of our Mother. The tall thin smart beauty with the "good hair" they made fun of. His

Demon Seeds

Mother hated our Mother, the Woman with the changing eyes from dark brown to light brown, whom Men would stare at. The eyes our Mother gave us. His Mother hated our Mother, despised her light, despised her charisma even through beatings, despised her "get back up again". My Father's Mother hated our Mother so much she trained her own kids and grandkids to hate my Mother, and in turn to despise us. You see, they loved the part of us that came from my Dad; so long as we were down and out or going through something.

They were fine with us but as soon as we were blessed with something good or descent they would find a way to destroy it or not celebrate it. Yes, my Grandmommy hated my Mother and so she hated us.

This particular day, we were dropped off a little earlier than usual. I hated going over to her house because I knew how she was going to treat us. My Mother came in saying she was going to work. She was explaining how she was excited about her new job. Grandmommy didn't care; in fact, she made sure that she did not respond to my Mom. She did not give her any praise, at all. Pretty soon, I saw my Mommy drop her head and say, "Ok well…I will see you later." My Mommy kissed me on the forehead and left to go to work.

I watched her through the screen, and I wanted to tell her how pretty she looked. I wanted to tell her that she "didn't need" Grandmommy's approval or anyone else's approval because she was a beautiful, tall fabulous woman with wonderful hair that I loved to touch.

After Mommy left, Grandmommy began her mental games with us. "You three...your parents never bring any food for you all...they never give me any money for taking care of you either...I can't stand your mom....she thinks she is soooo pretty...hmph...she's too skinny...and irritating...no wonder your Dad knocks her in the head...I am by myself...I don't have any food to feed you all..."

I was crying...I hated what she said about my Mother and I hated her...at least at that moment.

As the day went on my cousins began to show up. Other parents dropped off their kids daily. My Mother hardly ever had money...but we paid for it every time. The other children were greeted with hugs and kisses and given cookies and candy. My cousin Sephora would taunt us with it. "You can't have none." My cousins Kate and Katrina, however, would sneak us some of whatever they were given.

Demon Seeds

This particular day, all the kids were sitting at the table eating lunch when my Aunt Deena walked in. "Hi baby!" She loved us. "How come ya'll not eating?" I was afraid to say anything, but my cousin Kate said, "Their Momma didn't bring any food, so Grandmommy said she wasn't gonna feed them!" Aunt Deena said, "Aw hell naw...Momma!!" She yelled at Grandmommy in the kitchen. "Why ain't you feedin' Charles and Fleta's kids?" Grandmommy looked guilty..."I was gonna feed them...eventually." "Momma its 4:00 and you ain't fed those kids all day? Momma what's wrong with you?!! Are you making the kids pay for something their parents do?!! You wrong Momma!!"

Aunt Deena motioned us to the table. "Come on kids." She had made us plates while she was talking. "Come sit at this table and eat." My cousin Kate smiled at me. I would always remember her for that.

After we ate, Grandmommy would walk by us and mumble things. She wouldn't say it loud enough for us to hear, but she gave us looks like the witch gave to Hansel and Gretel. She wanted us dead.

I did not find out until later that the reason Grandmommy treated my Mother so bad had to do with a family historical event. Turns out my Grandfather,

Grandmommy's husband, had a crush on my Mother's Grandmother. Johnnie Lucille was my Great Grandmother's name and she was a beauty. She was a very classy woman who always carried a matching purse, gloves and shoes.

She was 5'4, could charm men with her smile and could win over the toughest customer. She was genuine and caring and people loved her. I studied her in hopes to be just like her some day. One day, when she was riding around town with us, my Father suggested we go to Grandmommy's house. My Mother was quiet, but my Nanna said, "Yes, I would love to sit with your Mother." We arrived and my Grandfather was sitting on the porch like he usually did on the weekends. My Grandmommy came out on the porch also and only saw our car and immediately her face had a scowl on it.

She looked like she'd seen a ghost when my Nanna stepped out of the car. I smiled to myself...I had never seen her scared. My Grandfather saw her too...He stood up and began to run...He ran through the yard...He ran down the walkway and he ran through the dirt to get to her as soon as he could. When he was in front of her he whispered, "Johnnie...Oh my God." He grabbed her hand and put it on his arm like he was escorting a debutante.

Demon Seeds

When we got to the porch he smiled at Grandmommy and said, "Johnnie's here." He sounded like a little boy with a crush. My Nanna hugged my Grandmommy before she could think about it. She said, "You look so beautiful...I am so glad to see you." Grandmommy was still standing there with her mouth open when I walked past her. Usually I never said anything to her, but today I said, "Hi Grandmommy!" She whispered, "Hi baby," but kept staring across the street.

During the visit, my Grandfather would run into the kitchen and refresh my Nanna's drink. He would hinge on her every word and tell her how beautiful she was. Nanna was holding my Grandmommy's hand the whole time and talking to her about what a wonderful woman she was and how God would bless her if she would only allow him to do so.

My Grandfather suggested taking my Great Grandmother out, but she looked at Grandmommy and said, I would never do that to another Woman, especially a Woman that I care about.

My Grandmommy's eyes began to water. She knew that Nanna could take her Husband if she wanted to, but she had chosen the path of respect and honor.

She also asked my Grandmommy to look after her Great Grandchildren and she told Grandmommy that she trusted her to do so. I was thinking, "oh no Nanna, don't trust her...she hates us!" I never said that of course.

Whatever was said...Grandmommy began to treat us differently. She would hug and love us and began to feed us often. It was like all of a sudden we became her favorites. She even told me I "looked like my Daddy" which hurt my mother, but it was her way of saying that we were accepted in the family. She would still say and do things to make my Mother cry, but now it came with..."The only reason I am doing this is because of Johnnie."

My Nanna was my Great Grandmother. Her name was Johnnie Lucille Austin and she chose to stay home and take care of her Mother while her two sisters, Jessie and Ritchie, decided to go to college. Nanna was the tiniest of the three Sisters and was taught very early in her life to iron and clean. As a young girl she taught me how to wash clothing using a washboard like the old 1940's easy ringers. She told me, "even though these fancy washing machines are being made you need to know how to wash things by hand."

As a little girl of age 8, I thought it was fun to help her wash clothes in the bathtub and to pour in the soap and bleach. Rinsing them out and ringing them out by hand. She would hum her favorite gospel songs as we worked. That's how I learned them…"the blood that gives me strength from daaay to daaay, it will ne-evah lose its power". That song was my favorite and still is my favorite today. She would tell me stories about Her Mother and that she was a classy woman who dressed well from the Goodwill and could sew up something wonderful.

Her Daddy was a hardworking man and dressed to the nines when he would take her Mom out on the town. He had come into this world as a slave and so had her Mom, but they were freed. She said she was from Birmingham Alabama, but we were told she was actually born in Jackson, Georgia. She said she began learning how to clean as soon as she could stand on a chair and do dishes. She knew that she was being prepped to be the one who stayed home. Her Sisters were sent to school and then to college. Nanna was sent to school, as well, but was taught the domestic side of life. She was to clean homes, become a maid and do the work of the church. She grew up Baptist but changed to the Seventh Day Adventist church by the time I was born.

As a young girl, I helped her wash the shirts the men would bring over to her home. "Make sure to run the wash soap over the collar and rub it together. That will get the ring out of it. Do the same for the under arms of the shirts." "Yes ma'am." I was humming songs with her..."Leaning, Leaning, Leaning on the everlasting arms..."

I would rub the underarms of the shirts and scrub the collars. The shirts were then placed in a bathtub half full of water and boxed bleach. It was hot and sometimes my hands would turn red, but I became immune to the heat quickly. We would do the same for our white undergarments; but washed them separately, of course. Then we would wash, rinse and wring them out in the machine. Nanna would hang them on a wire hanger in the bathroom and pull the bottom of the shirts to try and get out as many wrinkles as possible.

Throughout the night we could hear the shirts dripping into the bathtub. It bothered me at first, but Nanna said the "bleach was cleaning out the bathtub, the drain and the air so that any dirty smells or bugs would be gone out of there by morning. "She said, "Roaches and bugs don't like the smell of bleach." As if Roaches were in a league of their own.

By morning the shirts were bone white clean and ready for ironing. We would pull them off the hangers and lay them on the couch so she could iron them. She had a mixture of the boxed starch and water that she would put in a bowl and then sprinkle it on the shirt with her fingers. It seemed she knew just the right amount to put on her hand. She had me try it a few times, but I always added too much. She would smile and giggle when I did it and just redo the part I had messed up.

She told me to start with the sleeves and then do the collar. Man, her stuff was crisp and the creases in those shirts walked down the street by themselves. She then taught me to iron the left side, the right side, and then the back of the shirt. I liked the smell of the starch and the crisp way the shirt felt after it was ironed. We would talk and laugh and share stories. She would tell me stories about my Mom and her siblings and my Grandma. They were mostly funny. She celebrated family adversity by laughing about it later and would give the perpetrators a family nickname, based on the issue. Example: When my Uncle fell on his face on the dance floor at a club called Simmons she gave him the nickname "Bo Diddly". When my Uncle Wade accidently smacked the flour and it blew up in his face she called him "Casper". She would keep that nickname for them forever until they had done something else to change it.

My nickname was Poopsie. Although I heard it was from my Grandpa Sam, Nanna tells me that my Mother said when

I was little. I did not like to be wet or be in a messy diaper; so, I would simply take it off and leave it wherever it dropped and keep on walking. Now that didn't mean that I had stopped the bodily function. So, I would leave quite a few remnants throughout the house.

The smell of the starch and the bleach brought memories. We would break and have a bologna sandwich and then go back to work. When I was old enough to truly know how to iron I would help her, and we would start in the morning and be done by Sunday night.

A few white men would come by and pick up their shirts and although she would charge them only $20 most gave her $100 or more. There was only one Black Pastor who came to her for his shirts, but in exchange he would have a group of deacons clean and weed her yard. They came every week, about five of them.

Nanna was beautiful, so a few of them would flirt with her from time to time. She always had water, lemonade and sandwiches ready for them whenever they finished. She would invite them in, and they would pray and sit and laugh with her for a few hours. We were never allowed into adult conversations, so I would sit in her room and pretend I was reading... hanging on every word. While she was talking with them, I would sit at her vanity. It was Victorian Versailles style. There were little bottles of perfume everywhere. Some of the bottles were full, some with just a drop and some were half full. I would sit and open them and smell them, pretending to be a rich Woman from Paris. They were from the 30s, 40s. I am not sure where they came from, but they were beautiful to me.

    I would look at myself in the mirror and remember my Aunt Norina saying how black, ugly and skinny I was; but then I remember my Nanna and My Mom describing me in quite a different way. As I looked at my image, I remember my Grandmother telling me I had beautiful thick hair and how wonderfully it would hold a press and curl. My Mother always said she was jealous of my eyebrows because they were naturally formed above my eyes. My Nanna loved my almond shaped eyes and my Mother loved my little nose. They both complimented my lips and cheeks and said those two items, along with my chin, were from them. My color was chocolate and they both loved that. It made me love being a chocolate girl. They never said anything negative about any other color, just that the color I had was the perfect color for me.

Charismatic Violence

Nanna told me during one of our ironing sessions that her Sisters were dark chocolate like her Father, and she was more cocoa. She believed they did not care for her for that and that her Father treated her better than them for that. Although she could not control how her Father felt, she wished and prayed God would change the heart of her Sisters. I only remember seeing Nanna's Sisters twice, maybe three times and two of the times I saw them, they made her cry.

She said she was always treated like she was beneath them by "them". Her Mother and Father held her close and she knew it. Because she chose to help take care of her parents, and especially her Mother. When she grew sick, she was closer to them.

Nanna was married at an early age to a man named Peterson and they had a boy first, whom she lost, and then a girl who I was blessed to call Grandma. She stayed with Peterson for a while but when she found out he was cheating she divorced him. She divorced him during a time when it was not acceptable to divorce a man and so she was scorned. It not only affected my Nanna, but my Grandmother informed me that she was made fun of at school. It was because of this divorce that my Nanna and my Grandmother did not get along. My Nanna felt like my Grandmother blamed her for sending away her Father and my Grandmother felt like she was light bright like her Father so that my Nanna did not like her.

Their interactions were always intense but mostly disrespectful. They found reasons, that were wrong with each other every time. It was scary to watch. They would laugh about me. Whenever they shared stories about interactions with me they seemed to come together, and I would try to find ways to get them there; often I would tell them both at the same time I loved them. They didn't hug or tell each other they loved each other. Most times my Grandmother would walk out angry.

My Nanna was very active in her Seventh Day Adventist Church in Pueblo, Colorado and she would often testify about her two marriages and how the first man gave her a venereal disease, so she divorced him; but how much she loved Austin, her second Husband. He was a Navy man and she had a picture of him sitting on a boat with his shirt off. She said he was killed during the war. She would cry at first, but then get this smile on her face. She said it every time she smiled, "Girl! If you ever experience a dark chocolate man, you won't want anythang else! Making love to a dark chocolate man is one of the most wonderful things you can ever do! Of course, I would make sure you are married first." She shuddered and walked into the kitchen giggling. She would tell us how "Austin" loved her better than any man ever had.

Nanna would tell us about how she took care of her Mother while she was sick, but never told us how she died. She would just say she became ill. She said her parents died, one after the other; but she did not tell me a time frame.

There is a picture she gave me of her Family, and I noticed her Father was dark chocolate. I knew her Father had been a model example for his Daughter and he just happened to be dark chocolate.

MOM ON DRUGS

I heard what I thought was a rat in the kitchen. I never really slept sound. As I walked in the dark, the sound of chewing got louder. What in the world was that sound?

As I came around the corner I could see a body bent over. There was a dripping sound like a leaky faucet. I turned on the light to see My Mother bent over biting the edge of a wood table. What in the world was she doing. I called her name, "Mom?" She jumped onto the kitchen table. Her voice was really low, "They are coming."

I said, "Who is coming Mom?" She had crouched down. She wasn't looking directly at me, but toward the kitchen cabinet. There was saliva and blood coming out of her mouth. Her teeth were bleeding. "The vampires...they are coming to get me. I am ready to go...to be a vampire." Suddenly she looked directly at me. "You should come too." Her eyes were piercing. Still crouching, she leaned to me. I was scared to death, but something wouldn't let me show it to her.

I told Her, "Mom you can't go, because I need you." She continued to stare at me….a blank stare…non-blinking. I lifted my hand up to her, "Come down Mommy." She was still staring at me…not blinking at all. I knew she was on drugs. I was to overhear my Dad laughing about her later. He was telling someone on the phone. "Fleta was trippin! I gave her some acid and she started thinking she was a vampire, so I dropped her ass off at home and went and did what I had to do."

I was still terrified when she grabbed my hand. She sat down on the table and then slid off. She stood in front of me. Not blinking. She wiped her mouth and chin on her sleeve…still staring at me.

All I could remember was to say what my Great Grandmother had told me to say when I suspected the devil was around, "Get thee behind me Satan." My Mom raised her eyebrows. I said, "In the name of Jesus." My Mom began to fall to the floor. I caught her and didn't even stumble. She was probably one hundred pounds. She wasn't allowed to gain weight, or my Father would use it as an excuse to beat her.

Mom on Drugs

Without thinking about the weight, I carried her to her bed.

I knew I was strong, but I didn't know why. I put her in her bed and put the covers over her. I knelt down beside her and asked God to protect her from the vampires and also to protect us.

AUNT BREANNA

We were at Aunt Breanna's house. My Father had just packed up a few clothes for us and said, "You are going to your Aunt Breanna's house for the summer." We loved our cousins Rose, Betsy and Andrew; so, we knew this was going to be a fun trip. It was late at night, so we slept most of the way. I remember watching the trees on the way to Denver and thinking how they looked like scary long-armed creatures. Always trying to grab at the car but we were too quick for them to grab.

I smelled marijuana. It was choking us, and we were coughing. I tried to roll down my window a little to get some air. I saw my Father look back...he was laughing..."Are you getting a contact?" He rolled the window down a bit more..."Ok baby...Daddy would never try to make you guys use drugs if you didn't want to, but one day you may want to, and I will be ok with that."

Aunt Breanna

I laid my head back and fell asleep. I did not want to hear one of his life speeches. He continued to talk, and I drifted off to sleep. When we got there, Aunt Breanna met us at the door. She had Blankets and pillows on her couches and on the floor. She said her kids were asleep so we could sleep here for now. She pointed to the couches and floors. We made ourselves comfortable. I woke up to at least three roaches staring at me. "Ahhhhhh" I screamed and scared the crap out of my Brother and Sister.

"Sister!" my Brother yelled out. He always screamed that when he was scared. My little Sister yelled "What happened?" I told them that three roaches were staring at me. It was just then that we heard the herd coming downstairs. It was Andrew…"Aw hell…we see roaches here all the time…they're like family. They wave good mornin' and everything!" We all yelled "Yayyyyy." We began to hug each other and say, "what's up" and everything else. We loved this set of cousins. They accepted and loved us for who we were, and they always had an adventure for us. We couldn't wait to play.

Aunt Breanna came out of her room in a robe. Uncle Kevin came out of his room in his robe and said, "Hey kids". He was always pleasant every time we saw him. Aunt

Breanna said she was going to make everybody breakfast. We went to the living room to watch Soul Train. We sat down to look at the television and then a big burly woman came out of Aunt Breanna's room in her robe. We looked at the kids…"Betsy said…oh that's Bunny. My Mom's girlfriend."

I looked at my Brother and Sister. Bunny said "Hey ya'll are some cute kids! Hi!" We were so starved for compliments…we said "Hiii." It sounded like a song.

We were to see Bunny a lot and she and Uncle Kevin seemed to get along. They were all about making sure Aunt Breanna was happy. Both Uncle Kevin and Bunny worked and paid bills and bought groceries. They would paint her toes and make her bath and run errands and pretty much do whatever she needed. It was during these times that we were left to fend for ourselves and that's what we did…we fended. There was not a lot of regular food in the house, so often we would find moldy bread or old potatoes to cook if they were on one of their three-day closed room fun events.

Betsy, Rose and Andrew taught us to pull off the moldy part of the bread on those days and to cut around the old parts of the potatoes. It was during the three-day events that I would watch my bowel movements. There would be moving worms in my stool. Sometimes during those days, I could feel the worms moving in my stool.

In the middle of the summer I told Aunt Breanna that I had little worms in my stool sometimes; and she said,"Oh hell! Ok, don't tell your Daddy and I will make sure it doesn't happen." She said,"Oh hell again." My Aunt Breanna made us all eat this chocolate bar stuff and we were all in the bathroom the whole day. A whole bunch of worms came out that day and I never had that happen again.

On one of our three-day weekends I left with Rose and she said, "Have you ever had a boyfriend?" I said, "No." She said, "Well, I think it's time for me to get you one." Apenimon. That was his name, but we and his family called him Apey. Pronounced App –eee. He was a little taller than I, with deep olive skin and long black hair. His eyelashes went on forever. I have always loved men with long eyelashes. Apey loved everything about me. He was the first of the male species to ever tell me that my skin was beautiful. The first day I met him, my cousin Rose walked in Ape's house and said, "Here she is you guys…my cousin…the pretty one I was talking about."

Ape's mom said…"oh she is pretty…" She said something in native American and smiled. She walked up to me and hugged me. His sisters hugged me too. My cousin Rose yelled "Apee come down here!!" I heard the sound of feet coming down the stairs. He had his hair pulled back in a ponytail. It was thick and long down his back. He was so handsome!! I was thinking how he would never like me. A flat chested seventh grader ...oh no...this guy was too wonderful.

When he saw me, he smiled. His teeth were perfect, and I had to wear a retainer. He said something in native American and then he grabbed my hand. Apey pulled me to him and said..."You are very beautiful. I love your chocolate skin." He was the first man to ever say my skin was beautiful. He kept touching my face and rubbing on my arm..."So soft"...."beautiful". During the rest of the visit Apey would take my hand and lead me around. He led me to the dinner table, he led me back to the couch in the living room and sat on the couch with me, holding my hand.

We talked about my home in Pueblo and why I was in Denver. We talked about his Native American heritage and why the earth was so important to him. We talked freely and with flow, during the whole visit. Rose was upstairs hanging out with Apey's Sister and a Spanish girl named Yvonne. I thought it was cool that we had the same name and spelled the same.

Aunt Breanna

When it was time for us to go home Apey said he would walk with us. Rose walked and laughed with Apey's sister and Apey, holding my hand of course, walking and continuing to tell me how beautiful I was. When we arrived home, I was scared because it was 11:00 at night and I thought we were going to get a whipping for coming in so late. Rose started laughing. She said, "They don't care...believe me...they don't even know."

Apey and I sat on the porch. He asked me if he could give me a kiss. I told him I didn't really know how to kiss, except for this one guy named Dennis but it was a quick peck.

Apey said..."I will teach you. Just do what I do." Apey placed his lips on mine and then showed me how to slowly open my mouth and how to gently bite a lip. He taught me how to kiss with my tongue and do it so passionately and slow that the other person would melt.

For the rest of the summer Apey would come to Aunt Breanna's door in the morning. He would always bring a flower or something to eat. He would draw me pictures of horses or the sun or the earth. He would sing native American songs to me. At some point in the morning everyone would leave, and wherever I was going, so was Apey. He would stare at me all day and hold my hand...sometimes he would even lotion my hands for me. We kissed constantly. We held hands and he always pulled me close.

We talked about having sex only once and I told him that I was not going to lose my virginity until after I graduated high school. He said ok.

On the day my dad showed up to pick us up Apey introduced himself to my Dad. He said "Hello Mr. York...My name is Apey and I love your daughter. When I grow up I am going to marry her." My Father was in a good mood and smiled and said, "Well what does Yvonne think?" Apey looked at me for affirmation. I said, "Dad I want to marry him too." My Dad laughed out loud and said, "Ok you two, then I am good with it."

My Father, My Aunt Breanna, My Uncle Kevin and Bunny all laughed. As we drove home I thought about all I had learned that summer. I now knew what sex was because my cousins had snuck into Aunt Breanna's room and stole her sex videos. Sex books and magazines were everywhere with all kinds of pictures of everything. Her kids, my cousins, were always sneaking into her room. They showed me pictures of her and Uncle Kevin and all the toys they had in their room. Their room always smelled like body or whatever that was.

She was nice to us and we never suffered any physical sexual abuse. She tried to hide it from us and her kids, but we knew what the visits were for and often strange people, couples and Women would come out of that room in the mornings. Aunt Breanna was free with her body, but you had to understand her story to understand why.

When Aunt Breanna was fourteen she was walking home from a friend's house late at night. She had to cross the ditch to get to the east side of town, and so she did. She didn't see the older Mexican man until he was standing right in front of her. He was drunk but was telling her how beautiful and chocolate she was. She was curvy for fourteen. Busty and curvy. The Mexican man spoke to her in both Spanish and English as he edged closer to her. He was successful in grabbing her, and as he raped her he beat her. She was screaming, but no one heard her, and he thought when he was done that he had killed her. She lay still with blood all over her face and clothing.

God woke her up. She could see the blue sky with all the stars Colorado is famous for, and she thought, I have to get home before I get in trouble. She tried to walk but could not stand up. Her pelvis felt crushed. She began to crawl. She crawled through the mud and the stream. She crawled up the side of the hill...blood from her body trailing behind her like a path to redemption. She crawled through stickers and dried crab grass. Her knees getting cut. She crawled through the school playground and onto the cement. The whole time thinking..."I don't know what I'm gonna tell Mama". She could see the lights from the house across the street. She was almost home.

She crawled all the way to the front steps. Up the front steps and lay at the front door. She stretched her hand to the screen and knocked as hard as she could.

My Grandmommy came to the door and screamed bloody murder at the sight of her daughter. She had her other children helped her with their Sister. They lay her on the couch and the girls immediately began to prepare a bath. My Grandfather was called at the mill where he worked. It only took him seven minutes to get home. He was covered with soot but fell to his knees when he saw his daughter. My Grandfather was a tall man. A Golden Gloves boxer and respected man in Pueblo. He had done a lot of favors for people in town and so the town looked out for him. The news spread fast in Pueblo about my Aunt Breanna and people began to come over with food and blankets and anything that would help her feel better or help my Grandmommy to get strength.

A phone call came to the house. A man from a bar called Simmons. That was the bar in Pueblo where everyone hung out. Generation after Generation. My Grandmommy called my Grandfather to the phone. The voice on the other end said..."Hey Lou...there's a Spanish guy here braggin bout havin' sex with a young black girl. He sayin' she was a sweet tender thang, but he knew she wanted it, so he gave it to her hard."

My Grandfather asked my Aunt Breanna if she was up to showing him if this guy was the one and she said, "Yes Daddy".

Everyone, including the children jumped in the car and headed to Simmons. My Grandfather instructed his family to stay in the car with the exception of Aunt Breanna. She held onto his hand and he was patient as she walked slowly and painfully into Simmons. The guy was at the bar laughing loud and still bragging about his conquest. My Aunt Breanna winced and looked up at her Daddy and said, "That's him, Daddy'"

Grandfather walked Aunt Breanna back to the car and instructed my Grandmommy to take the kids home and wait for him to arrive. Grandmommy couldn't drive, so Lee drove them home.

She winced and headed home with the kids. My Grandfather walked back into the bar and told the bartender to call the police. The police knew my Grandfather and they certainly did not want any trouble from him or he from them.

When the police arrived, Grandfather met them outside. He told them what had happened to Aunt Breanna and they said they would bring the man outside.

The police brought him outside and explained he was under arrest for the rape of a minor. The man was laughing until he was escorted to the alley behind the bar. My Grandfather came out of the shadows. The Mexican man was introduced by the police to my Grandfather. "This here is the Father of the little girl you raped. He wants to talk to you." The police told my Grandfather he had ten minutes. They walked to the street to talk.

My Grandfather used all the power in his golden glove hands to beat the man senseless; and my understanding is the man was a vegetable after that and remained in the Pueblo state hospital until his death.

MENTALLY TIRED

According to history, the Pueblo State Hospital housed a few family members. My Mother in a mental institution – I didn't know until I was in high school that the summer I was at Aunt Breanna's my Mother was in the Pueblo State Hospital. Apparently she was there with my Aunt El.

My Mother had snapped when my Dad took us. He had told my Mom he was going to kill us and that she would never see us again. She thought he had finally done it, killed her Children. I am certain she broke down because she loved her kids. My Aunt Norina, of course, was laughing about it.

She didn't know I was standing around the corner from them. She didn't know I was on the other side of the wall thinking about how cruel they were not to help my Mommy find us. How mean they were knowing we were with Aunt Breanna and letting my Mom go crazy. I knew they would reap what they sowed.

GROCERY STORE REALITY

Look up Mommy! We were in the grocery store and my Mom had her head down. It was like she was worn out. She was giving me directions. "Baby, grab that spaghetti right there" or "Grab that peanut butter for Mommy". She kept her head down and her brunette wig covering her forehead and her face.

She was badly beaten. The thing is...she had covered up the bruises very well with make up and although the scars were underneath she was still beautiful, but did not know it.

She asked me to grab the Captain Crunch from the shelf and when she did I said, "Look up Mommy, you are beautiful! Put your head up so people can see how pretty you are." My Mom gasped. It was like she had never heard that before. She kissed me on the forehead, and she said, "Ok baby, I will look up from now on."

She did too. She looked up and even smiled at people. When we reached the checkout, a woman touched my

Grocery Store Reality

Mother's hand and said. "I have been there...where you are. I have a number you can call to get help. A place you can go to get help for this. My Mom was shaking her head, "No...I can't. He said he would kill my parents."

I looked at my Mom and began to cry. I believe that was the first time I began to contemplate how to kill my Father.

ANNETTE

I think Momma let her in because she was a big woman and wore big glasses and had a pie face. Annette was there for my Mom or at least Mom thought she was. Annette had come to our door to use the phone. She had been in a car accident up the street and she needed to call the police. My Mom let her in and while Annette waited for the police they became friends.

Annette was a strait-laced Woman, no drinking, no drugs, no kids, and so she loved us. She would babysit us and buy groceries for my Mom. She would give my Mom money when my Dad took it away and she would take my Mom to get her hair done every so often.

She steered clear of my Dad because he would treat her bad...well at first. Understand that Men who are abusive generally want to isolate their Women. He would stomp around and slam things when Annette came over. She would get nervous and hug my Mom and then leave. Annette

Annette

quickly figured out that my Dad would not hit my Mom when she was there. So passively aggressively she would hang out with my Mom until my Dad left to go do whatever it was he was going to do.

My Dad soon figured this out. He took another route. He knew that Annette was insecure about her looks and my Mom was just insecure and so he began the game. He began to invite Annette to dinner and would compliment my Mom and Annette on a true friendship.

I remember the night things began to change. My Father put on his old school music and then offered Annette and my Mom a glass of wine. My Mom took the wine as to not anger my Dad and Annette, following her lead, took a glass as well.

They began to get drunk. My Dad was giving my Mom tequila and giving Annette wine. Pretty soon Mom was passed out on the couch and Dad began to play slow songs. He pulled Annette up to him and began to tell her how pretty she was. He was telling her how he preferred big women and that he was only mean to my Mom because he hated that she was "so damn skinny".

He told Annette, "You're beautiful you know that?" She was giggling and letting my Dad dance and sing to her. He tried to kiss her, and she pulled away. "No Charles...Fleta is my friend."

She grabbed her purse from the couch and walked out.

I closed the door to my room and climbed into bed.

After that night my Dad would talk to my Mom about Annette all the time. My Mother's defense mechanism was to then begin dogging Annette. She figured if she pointed out Annette's flaws then my Dad would not want her. but he was on a mission.

Annette was a big, thunderous Woman. 6' tall and big all over. She was square shaped and probably wore the biggest, roundest glasses the eighties could offer...they were Elizabeth Arden... and Annette felt like the glasses and her bangs with a bob hairstyle at least made her look decent.

She told my Mom that she was not attractive on every occasion. In her deep voice, she would make fun of herself. Laugh about her big nose and big breasts that got in the way of everything.

My Mom thought she was a safe friend because of her unattractiveness and my Dad had begun to agree with my Mom. One day my Dad asked where Annette worked.

Annette

Subsequent to that, Annette still would come by and check on my Mom but instead of defending my Mom she began to make excuses for my Dad.

I remember wanting to say to my Mom that the tide had shifted, and she should be careful what she told Annette from here on out, but I didn't.

One day Dad came home and had this look on his face. He walked in and said, "ummmhmmm."

My Mom stood up and said, "Hi baby" and leaned over to kiss him. In front of us, he slapped her so hard she fell and broke the table.

"You been telling Annette about my business…about my family? How you hate my family? Is that what you been sayin?"

Mom was stunned, she was crawling backwards on her hands and feet. He looked up at us, "Get in your rooms!" We ran to our rooms. He beat her for about two hours and then he told her to call Annette. He told her to tell Annette he wasn't there and that she needed to talk to her. Mom called Annette and when she hung up the phone he picked up the receiver and began to wrap the phone around her neck. He yelled for us to come out into the living room. He was choking her and making her look at us. He asked us, "When me and your Mom break up do you want to live with me or her?"

I was shaking my head no. I did not want to answer. My Brother and Sister were looking up at me for the answer. He was pulling the cord harder now, "WHAT THE F**K ARE YOU KIDS GOING TO DO!!?? Stay with me or go with your Mom!?"

I said, "Go with you, go with you."

He dropped her and the phone on the floor. "See Bi**h. These kids don't care about you!" He had his back turned and was in the refrigerator.

My Mom looked up at me and nodded her head. She was letting me know that I had done the right thing.

When Annette arrived, we were all sitting on the couch. He had made all of us sit there and wait for her.

She walked in and was surprised when my Dad came out of the kitchen. It was the first time I saw her scared.

He lit a joint and said to my Mom, "So this is your friend?"

She was crying. He went and stood in front of her and yelled, "I SAID IS THIS YOUR F**KING friend??!!"

Annette

She nodded yes. He looked at Annette, "Are you her friend?" Annette whispered, "Yes." She looked at the floor.

He started laughing. "Awwww this fat b**ch! You are not HER friend!" He was pointing at my Mom. You ain't nobody's friend! You are just a b**ch I used to get information on Fleta!" He was laughing at Annette.

"I slept with you yesterday and this morning just to prove to Fleta that you were the low life hoe I knew you were!"

He bent down in front of her, "You thought I was going to really leave my wife and kids? For you? That is never going to happen!! My wife is the real deal! Beautiful! Amazing! (Mom lifted up her head to look at him)

"Sh*t! My wife is beautiful and smart! And look at my kids! My kids are beautiful! What in the hell would make you think that I would leave my wife and have porky a** kids by you?! By your fat a**!!"

My Brother giggled. My Dad looked at him, "YOU can laugh son! She will never mess up my family!" My Dad motioned my Mom to come to him. She stood up and limped over to him. He kissed her on the forehead, her blood now on his lips, "Baby, tell her to get the f**K out of our house. Tell Her!!"

Mom yelled at Annette, "Get out of our house, b**ch!"

Annette who had paid our rent in the past, who had stood up for my Mom, who had picked us up from school realized that she had been used, played like a fiddle. She stopped at the door and turned to my Mom, "I will still come if you need me, I am so sor..." She didn't get it out. My Dad kicked her, and she fell out of the front door.

In the sickness of the situation, we used this to get him on our side. We clapped and he bowed. "I love you guys, hell, I ain't going to leave my family! Not for that!" As kids, we hugged our Dad. He had defended us and we all now had an enemy together. I ran to get my Mom a washcloth so she could wash her face. She was smiling as he was talking about how he had slept with Annette and all of the things he had made her do to him because she was insecure. I was setting the table and Dad said, "Let's all eat together tonight at the table." He would compliment Mom all night and we would use this story for at least 6 months to keep him from hitting her. Whenever he seemed mad, we would bring up how he "got Annette straight that one night". It worked for a little while.

SEXUAL LEARNING

One day, My Father was angry about my being in the bathroom so long. Being sixteen, I was trying to understand the shape of my body. Figuring out whether or not my body was a good one or not. I would stand in the mirror and stare at myself, wondering if my breasts were big enough or if my body was curvy enough. I would even look at my butt and wonder if it was big enough.

The guys at school would tell me I was fine, but honestly I could not figure out where or how. I blew the compliments off most of the time because I knew guys would say anything to get sex; and besides, I was dedicated to Reggie my boyfriend.

On this particular day I had just taken a shower. I was on my period, so I took longer than usual. My Father startled me by banging on the door. "What the hell are you doing in there!" My Mom was not home, so I became his target. "Dad, I was taking a shower because I am on my period."

He screamed, "You are on your period!!?? Get out here!" I hurried up, put my clothes on and came out of the bathroom. "Get downstairs in my room. I think you are curious about some shit and I am going to end this once and for all!!" I did not know what was about to happen, but I knew it wasn't right. When I walked into my Father's room he had put on his robe. He turned to me and told me to sit down on his bed. He began to tell me about how boys would say anything to get what they wanted, and he was going to show me what would happen if I ever was with a boy!!

He pulled out his erect penis and put it right in my face. I turned my head to look the other way. "Look at it!" I shook my head no. "Look at it or I will beat the hell out of you!" I looked at it. It was now about an inch from my face. "Now touch it!! Touch it!!"

I pulled my right hand up slowly and touched the tip with my five fingers. "Now wrap your hands around it!" I was crying, heaving and scared. He was screaming at the top of his lungs about sex, boys and my curiosity. I was a whore and I was going to be a whore so he might as well prepare me. I did what I was told. I had never actually seen a grown man's penis. Only my little brother's when I had changed him. I was scared. I was terrified. I was a virgin. Through tears I said,

Sexual Learning

"Dad, this is not right, and God doesn't like this." My Dad stopped screaming and was silent as if someone had physically grabbed his tongue.

I still had my hand wrapped around his penis.

"Get the f**k outta here!" I ran upstairs to my room and started crying. I locked my door and curled up under the covers in my bed. When my Mom came home she knocked on my door. My Dad had of course told her his version of the story and left the house.

I shared with her the truth and expected her to be mad. She wasn't. When my Dad came home we were all sitting at the dinner table. He sat down next to the wall and told her to fix his plate right now. She put chicken on his plate and then sent the plate like a Frisbee towards his head. We were all astonished at what happened next.

Mom spun that plate like a professional baseball player. My Father moved just in the nick of time. The plate whizzed past him...and stuck in the wall behind him, some of the chicken still on it. We were all staring at Mom with our eyes popping out. My Dad stood up and didn't say anything. He moved slowly towards the living room.

Charismatic Violence

My Mother turned around slowly with the biggest butcher knife I have ever seen, held firmly in her hand. She looked up over her eyes at my Father...she looked possessed. In her lowest, manliest voice I would ever hear, she began to speak slowly and methodically, "If ...you...ever...make my daughter...touch you again...I will kill you...I will cut your throat in your sleep."

Generally, my Father would slap her down. Generally, my Father would have walked up to her and taken the knife or called her out of her name...but today he backed away slowly. He picked up his keys and his coat and slowly backed out of the front door. He was gone for at least two weeks.

When my Dad came home he apologized and explained there was a reason for what he had done. He was trying to scare me and there was a reason why.

Previous to the penis incident, My Father came home from work slamming the front door! "Yvonne" he screamed. He was yelling at the top of his voice. I ran up the stairs. "Yes sir!" He was screaming in my face. "Have any of my brothers or your uncles ever touched you or tried to sleep with you!!"

I was thinking..."he is really crazy". I yelled back..."Dad, God no! None of my uncles have ever done anything like that to me!!" He was still yelling, "Ok, well if they ever do, damn it I will kill them. Dead, damn it. I'll die and go to hell before anyone ever touches my daughters." I didn't understand at the time what was going on, but I was to find out later that my Father was escalated because of something he had found out about my Uncle Zeke. Here we go...another elephant...wasn't this family tired of not being able to breathe in the room? The elephants were suffocating us!!

Uncle Zeke had been sleeping with his daughters. One whom he'd slept with and then forced to have an abortion. Rumor was that she had a couple of abortions because of him. She was beautiful but very sexual and at an early age; and the behavior now, was understood.

My Uncle Zeke's daughters had been neglected from early on in their lives. We were witnesses to the crime.

BABYSITTING AND HAIRCARE

Loretta was one of Uncle Zeke's children. She was the light skinned one with pretty green eyes. She was exactly the opposite of her Sisters. They were dark, she was light. They had brown eyes, she had hazel. When she was four, her Mother Ellie did not have a babysitter in the summer. So, my Mother offered "my" babysitting services, which basically meant I was watching not only my brothers and sisters, but also an additional three children for a total of eight children, aged nine or younger.

I was twelve, responsible for feeding them, keeping them clean and making sure they stayed out of trouble. Although scary at times, I loved being in charge. Loretta's hair was curly tight, and her Mother did not know how to comb it; for that matter she really did not know how to do any of her daughters' hair. The first day she brought them over, all three smelled like urine. Their clothes looked like they had not been washed for a long time. Stains and dirt were all over everything. My baby Sister grabbed her nose, "Ew you guys smell like pee!" I shook my head at her and said, "That's not nice, Sister."

After all the parents left I went into the bathroom and began to run water for a bath. I knew the girls liked bubbles, so I put some Mr. Bubble in the tub. I made it a little warmer than warm to make sure the smell would go away.

As the water ran in the bathtub, I ran water in the sink. I put some tide in the sink and went to the girls. "Girls, come with cousin Von." They all followed me to the bathroom.

My brothers and sisters were being histrionic, holding their noses like they were dying of the smell as we walked by.

I told the girls to take off their clothes and get into the tub. They were more than happy to jump into the pink bubbles. While they played in the tub I took their clothes to the sink and soaked them in the water. The smell was rancid.

I went back to my bedroom and pulled out three of my T-shirts...yep that would work. It would cover them completely up. After laying the three T-shirts on the bed I went back into the bathroom. I began to wash them all over...hair...body and especially in their private areas. The youngest one began to cry. I asked her what was wrong, and she said..."I want to smell bad; I don't like it when I smell good."

I remember thinking..."she has always been weird'" I would find out later why she wanted to smell bad. I told the girls they could play awhile, and I would come back for them. I went to the living room to check on my brother and sister. They were watching Sesame Street, while sitting on the floor.

I went to the kitchen and began scrubbing the clothes between my hands like my Great Grandmother had taught me to. She had a scrub board we used to wash and clean shirts on when I went over her house. So, I used this method to clean the girls' clothes. My Nanna used to wash and starch shirts for a living and she wanted me to learn how to wash clothes by hand, just in case I did not have money to go to the Laundromat. She had no idea how many times I would wash clothes by hand after her training.

I washed and washed those clothes. I washed their little panties and took pride in them turning from gray with flowers to white with flowers. I ignored the streaks of urine and feces and just changed the water as often as necessary. I took them out of the sink turned them to wring them and then went to go get the girls out of the bathtub.

I pulled them out of the bathtub and told them to dry themselves off.

As they dried off I used the comet on the ring around the bathtub…I didn't want my Dad to beat up my Mom for the tub being dirty.

After the girls were dry I put Jergens lotion on them and put a big T-shirt on each of them and told them to sit down and watch TV with my brother and sister.

I knew they would be hungry, so I made peanut butter and jelly sandwiches for them and cut the sandwiches into sections of four.

I went back to the kitchen and began to rinse out the girls' clothes with warm water. I took them outside and hung them on the line in the backyard. Yards don't really have clothing lines in the back yard anymore, but it sure made the clothes smell fresh. I smiled when the sun came out because I knew the clothes would dry quickly.

The kids were done eating so I read a book to them and then made them practice one of the plays I made up. I made up plays to keep them busy and dancing. I knew that if I kept them dancing and moving then I would be able to sleep when they took a nap.

We performed made up plays...church plays, plays based on commercials, Disney plays...whatever it was that would keep them busy. Many times, we would mimic Sesame Street, electric company, zoom...whatever worked. When the kids would sleep I would clean and then sleep myself. They were not bad kids. They minded and they did what they were told.

Every Monday I would braid the girls' hair. It was always matted, and Loretta had hair "straight outta Africa" as I would call it. It was like mine, so I knew what to do with it. I washed it...covered it with Blue Magic and then braided it into four sections. Most times, I would connect the front two braids to the back two braids and call it done... By the end of the summer her hair had started to grow. I was proud of what I had done for them. I loved them. They were my family and I was going to be there for them, no matter what. We were to all grow up together.

Many years later, my brother came home from school and he was cussing and screaming. I went into my brother's room and asked, "What happened?" My brother told me he had trashed Uncle Zeke's house. Wide eyed I said..."Are you crazy??!!" He said, "Naw...you don't know what he did!" I

Babysitting and Haircare

asked, "WHAAAT??" My brother said, "He has been having sex with his own daughters!!! All this time! The oldest one has had two abortions from him! That's why the youngest one used to pee and doo on herself! Remember when she used to say she didn't want to smell good? Well that was why!"

I sat down on the couch. It all made sense now...the clothes...the smell. "Well, wait a minute", I looked up at my Brother..."What about their Mom?" "Oh, she knew, but she didn't do anything!" I began to cry..."Those poor girls...oh no...it is so not fair." I remember reaching out to the girls and letting them know I was there if they needed me. I wanted to always be there, that person in their family who supported them through it all. When we got older I was to find out that one of them had slept with my ex-husband and that the other had encouraged him to cheat on me.

I guess I should have been angry with them, but I wasn't. I already knew that they had self-esteem issues. I already knew my purpose for them when they were little, and I was upset with myself for not knowing that they were being abused. I was upset with myself for not knowing that they were getting spanked with all of their clothes off. Even I was upset!

I could only feel sadness in knowing that every night they must have felt scared to death...wondering which room he would come to. Knowing that their Mother knew and would do absolutely nothing.

As an adult, the oldest one began selling crack. She had been supplying it to her Father for free for years. My brother said he went to her and asked her..."Why are you selling that stuff to your dad? You shouldn't be doing that?" Her reply? "I am not selling it to him...I am GIVING it to him...as much as he wants... anytime he wants....I am hoping he dies!"

EVIL EDUCATION

This day I walked into the room and sat down on the couch. Behind us were the bay windows filled with potato plants. As I sat down with my Mom I noticed the pretty flowers in the middle of the grass on the mound. The outside always looked so well-groomed.

I had helped my Mom sit down. She was hurting...her whole body... and she moaned and grunted as she sat down. The left side of her face was swollen black and blue. She had a makeshift bandage on her head. Gauze over a head gash placed on her head with masking tape. The gauze was full of blood dried and new. I noticed a trail of blood running down the side of my Mother's face. I reached up with my eight-year-old fingers and wiped it away. I rubbed her blood on my jeans.

My Mother was looking at the floor. Submissive... mentally beat down and tired. I could hear them coming. She didn't look up. I did. I looked at all three of them. My Grandmommy, My Aunt Lorna and My Auntie Ariel.

My Grandmommy started it, as usual. "He is going to continue to beat you until you ack right. I hope he leaves a knot on the other side of your head!" My Mom continued to look down. My Auntie Ariel began…"You deserved this one because you are so stupid! You should never say anything when he is angry because then you make him angrier and then you get beat harder…You're stupid, but you deserved this one Fleta!" My Mother said nothing. My Aunt Lorna began…'I have always hated you. You are pathetic and I think you trapped my Brother! He deserves a better Woman than some common whore! Ew, you make me so sick just looking at you." My Mother kept looking down and said nothing. It was not until my Aunt Lorna turned to me that my Mother began to cry. "Your daughter is a little ugly black skinny child. She is so hideous! She looks like "your" side of the family!! She is so ugly and black!!"

My Mom began to sob. I could hear my Dad in the kitchen, laughing. He was acting as if nothing was going on in the kitchen. When my Mom began to sob, they walked away. Still talking about how stupid my Mom was. As they entered the kitchen, I heard my Dad say, "Well did ya'll talk to her?" My Grandmommy said in a gentle voice, "Yeah we talked to her, but I don't know if it did any good. She didn't even say anything. I don't think we can help her. You are just going to have to continue doing what you are doing." I watched them hug and kiss my Father and tell him that they loved him. They were telling him that they would support him anytime he needed them.

My Father walked through the hall and stood in front of my Mother. "Well" he said "They can't stand you and I can't stand looking at you! Get you're a** out of here and go sit in the car!" I stood up to try and help her up. He growled at me and gritted his teeth, "SIT DOWN AND DON'T YOU DARE HELP HER." I sat down. My Mom was moaning as she stood up. She made her way to the front door...when she got there he kicked her in the back, and she fell through the screen to the ground on the concrete porch.

My Aunt Lorna yelled, "Oh well!" My Mother gathered herself and made her way to the car.

My Dad stayed in the house another four hours. My Grandmommy made him a plate of food and he ate...in front of me, knowing that my Mother and I had not eaten all day. When it was time to go, he bent down to me and said..."You know why I didn't feed you?" I shook my head no. "Because

I am going to teach you that when you help your Mom you starve." Understood? "I said, "Yes sir." My Auntie Ariel chimed in 'Yea baby...just stay out of it. Your Daddy knows what he is doing. She kissed me on the cheek and put a Hostess Ding Dong in my pocket."

My Dad rubbed my head. "Go head baby you can eat it. You are good now." I immediately became an actress. "Thank you Auntie Ariel!" I jumped up and hugged her real hard. "You are the best Aunt ever." My Grandmommy and My Aunt Lorna...sang..."awwwww". I had won them over, if only for a moment.

"I want to save it for later to eat when I play dolls." My Dad said, "Okay baby, you do it your way." They were all so proud of themselves. I bolted out of the door and started skipping so they would think I was happy. I was going to save it for my Mom.

On the way home my Dad stopped at McDonald's. He bought me a kid's meal, and of course, nothing for my Mom. When we arrived home, he told my Mom to get out of the car. I was getting out also.

He rolled down the window. "I am going to spend the night with Lisa, and I might spend the weekend with her. Do you have a problem with that?" My Mother shook her head no.

He sped off. We went into the house and my Mother washed her face. When she came out I had set the table and divided the food in half. My Mother said, 'Baby, I am not hungry." I pulled a chair out from the table. "Mommy, I can't eat this by myself and I would feel really, really, really bad if you made me eat by myself."

She smiled. I had made her smile. "Ok baby."

When she sat down I prayed over the food and asked God to please heal my Mommy. She began to eat dinner, but I told myself I would talk to her and a lot so she would never feel bad about her pain. I told her that the people and the teachers at my school thought she was beautiful. She looked up at me. "Really?" I said, "Yes Mommy, and I do too."

Something happened to my Mom at that moment. She began to laugh and talk just as fast as I was. We giggled and she told me what a wonderful daughter I was to set the table. We read books that weekend and laughed together. It was just the two of us, since my Brother and Sister were staying the weekend with their friends.

I realized, at that moment, she had this fabulous bounce back quality. She was to pass this trait to me.

GETTING HIGH

It was my senior year in high school, and I had just turned eighteen. I came home and my Mom and Dad were downstairs and of course I could smell the weed when I walked in. I didn't want to go downstairs to the drugs and the company that was there on drugs. So, I yelled down, "Mom, Dad...I'm home!" My Dad said, "OK baby!" Then I heard the dreaded words. "Come down here...me and your mom want to show you something."

"Yes sir"...I was walking slowing into the mist of weed clouds and pissed off because I had to study, and I was hoping this would not make me high. When I got to the bottom of the steps there were little glad bags with different types of pills, weed and other stuff in them. It was spread all over the counter. My Father gave me a hug and motioned for me to sit at the bar. "Baby, me and your Mom think that because you're going to college we should tell you what all these drugs are so that nobody tries to trick you." I was thinking, "Really?" the philosophy of drugs? You gotta be kidding me?

He began to show me windowpane, heroine, crack, pills called Christmas trees and a whole slew of other things that he felt I should be aware of. He made sure to show me how to break down cocaine so that no one could poison me before I snorted it and then he and Mom showed me "how" to snort it. I refused of course. After my drug lesson I was tired and aggravated. I said, "Ok, well thank you for the lesson. I feel aware now." I headed toward the stairs. My Dad turned off the music. "Hey where are you going. It was that voice that meant he was getting mad and someone was going to get hurt. I said, "Dad, I have to study."

"Not now you don't…so you have a choice…you are going to have to take one of these drugs…I am not going to pick one for you but you are going to take one because me and your Mom need to know how you act when you are high, so you can't run game on us." I was bewildered…was this really happening? Was my Dad forcing me to take drugs? I looked at my Mom's face and she looked scared. I knew that if I refused a drug my Mom would get beaten up.

I walked over to the counter and tried to think about what I had learned in my sociology class about drugs and which one would create minimal distraction from my studies. I chose the marijuana and when my Father's back was turned my Mom pointed out the one that was less potent. My Dad was smiling, he was happy that I was going to take drugs. It was an evil smile and I hated him for it.

My Mother was crying and wiping the tears so my Father wouldn't see them. As my Father was rolling the joint he began singing one of the songs playing on the stereo. My Mom would smile at him so he would feel good and then he lit the joint. He made my Mother show me how to do it and so when I inhaled I coughed; but by the third puff I had mastered it. Very soon, I began to laugh, and everything was funny. The last thing I remember was laughing about the shape of people's ears. When I woke up it was two in the morning and I was downstairs in the basement. Someone had put a cover over me.

When I went to stand up, my head hurt like someone had put a hammer to it. I fell to my knees from the pain. I was whirling and it felt like I was on a merry go round and the pain was excruciating. I threw up and then fell in it. I was crawling, but I didn't know where I was going. I was trying to yell but couldn't and I felt like I couldn't breathe.

Getting High

Finally, my head felt so heavy that I could not lift it and I could not gasp for air. People may say I am crazy, but it was then that I thought I saw Jesus. He was in white, a cloud I think. In this vision, He bent down next to me and began to rub my forehead back to my hair. He did not say anything, but I knew he was there, letting me know that it was going to be ok. I figured if I was going to die then He would be there with me; so, it wasn't going to be so bad, plus maybe I would be out of this crazy house once and for all. I passed out.

I woke up covered in vomit. It was already 8:00 and I was going to be late for school. I ran to the shower and started the water. While the water was warming up I figured I would clean up the vomit with comet. It only took me about five minutes. My head was splitting, but I convinced myself I could do this. I jumped in the shower and then into my cheerleading uniform. Thank God I did not have to iron.

I ran to the bus stop and prayed that my teachers would not use this against me. When I was at the bus stop a guy pulled over who was probably about 25 and asked me did I need a ride. I told him "I do, and I am late, but I don't know you." He said, "I get that, but my name is Lanier and I won't hurt you. Here call my Sister." He had one of those huge cell phones and when his Sister answered the phone he said, "Sis, do you need me to take you anywhere today?" She said, "No Lonnie...you are so stupid, I have my own car! Why are you calling asking me that?" He looked at me and smiled, "OK?"

I don't know why I said, "OK". I got in and he took me to school. I got there on time with a few minutes to spare. "Can I get a number to call you?" Yes, I said and wrote down what I knew was the wrong number. "Should I call you tonight?" I smiled, "Sure, but after nine because I have a game". I knew he would be dialing a wrong number. He said, "You are so beautiful...I can't wait to talk to you tonight". I said, " I feel the same way and thank you for giving me a ride."

"Anytime beautiful"...he smiled.

As I got out of the car I looked again at his wedding band. I remember thinking to myself as I walked into the school. Game recognizes game.

SMOKEY ROBINSON

My Mother loved Smokey Robinson. She would play his albums all the time. The first time she bought one of his albums my Dad grabbed her by the throat and asked her why she would buy another Man's album when she had a man who could sing right in her own home. She was smart and said, "I bought his album because he sounds like you." Of course, that worked and from then on if my Father came home and heard Smokey Robinson playing he would start smiling because he thought my Mom was thinking about him. While we were living in California my Father had run into a man who claimed he was a talent agent. He had watched my Father at some club and then gave my Father five tickets to a concert. There were three singers. I cannot remember one of them, but I do remember Smokey Robinson and Stephanie Mills were going to be there. I remember my Mother stating that "Stephanie Mills was not attractive" but she would sit through her anyway.

I don't know where my Father got the money, but we went shopping that day. My Brother, Sister and I were given new clothing to wear and Momma was given a new dress. My Father was dressed to the nines as always and to anyone who saw us we were that night a "Handsome" family.

When we walked into the concert hall there were posters and T-shirts and albums available for purchase. Mom walked over to the table with the Smokey Robinson stuff. She wanted a T-shirt with fringe on it, but Dad bought her a long night shirt to sleep in. Smokey Robinson's eyes adorned it. Mom was okay with that. Anything she had to represent Smokey Robinson was okay with her.

I remember walking into the circle in the star music hall and looking up at the lights and the stage. Dad was in a good mood so I asked him, "Daddy, is this in a circle so people can see the person singing at all sides?" Daddy said to my Mother, "See she's smart like I told you." He looked down at me, "Yes baby and the stage moves real slow in a circle so the singer ends up singing to everyone in the room." I smiled up at him.

We found our seats and got ready for the show. Stephanie Mills was on first and I remember her voice making me cry because it was so beautiful. After Stephanie

Smokey Robinson

Mills completed her set my Mother bent over to me and said..."Wow she just became the most beautiful woman in the world". I nodded my head in agreement. My Sister and Brother were talking to each other. They were excited and pointing at lights and things in the concert hall.

It was then that the lights went down and all we heard was Smokey Robinson's voice. The women began to scream! The screaming was so loud Smokey Robinson had to ask the ladies to calm down so he could be heard performing. My Mother wasn't screaming, she was just holding her hands to her chest and crying. They were happy tears and as I looked up at her, I was happy for her. Smokey Robinson didn't move much on the stage, but he sang very well. My favorite song was "Quiet Storm".

Women were throwing bras and panties on stage and every so often Smokey Robinson would chuckle and watch the stagehands pick them up.

Then it got quiet and a man came on stage with a vase full of roses. Smokey Robinson was walking into the audience handing the women roses. We were sitting in the middle seats, so we did not expect Smokey Robinson to come all the way up where we were...but he did.

Smokey Robinson reached out to my Mother and took her hand. He lifted her up and told her she was beautiful. He asked my Father if he was her husband and my Dad said, "Yes". He asked my Father if he could have permission to dance with his wife and to give her a rose. My Father said, "Yeah sure!" He was on stage and played along because he knew the audience was looking at him. It was when he sat down that I knew. I knew my Mother would pay for this. He was out of the spotlight and was staring at my Mom with disdain. She was looking into Smokey Robinson's eyes and he was dancing with her, holding her close and singing to her. He then gave her a rose and gently sat her in her seat. She was a lady...even with Smokey Robinson she was not screaming and yelling or behaving badly. Smokey Robinson said, "Thank You" to my Father and went back to the stage. My Mom tried to hold my Dad's hand, but he snatched it away from her. She looked alarmed and confused. She looked at me with fear in her eyes and shrugged her shoulders. I shrugged mine back to her.

After the concert we headed back to the motel we were staying in. It was about one in the morning and we were all tired. When we parked in front of the hotel my Father instructed my Mom to go into the room. He began to lower the front seat back and the driver's seat back. He told me to get into the driver's seat and told my Brother to get into the passenger's seat. He told my Sister to lay down in the back seats. He told us he didn't have any blankets so we would have to put our coats over us to stay warm for the night, but we would be sleeping in the car tonight.

I remember being grateful to be able to get a good night's sleep. I knew he would be yelling at my Mom for the Smokey Robinson thing, so I was fine with sleeping in the car. After laughing and talking with my Brother and Sister we all fell off to sleep.

I woke up to my Dad opening up the car and grabbing me out of it by my arm. He nearly threw me to the ground. "Get out of the damn car!" He was yelling at the top of his voice. "All of you, get out of the car!" My Brother and Sister scrambled out of the car and as we were standing in the parking lot he screeched off and down the street!

When we walked into the room there was blood everywhere. I told my Brother and Sister to walk to the office and ask them for more towels. I did not see my Mom, but I already knew she was in the bathroom. When I went to push the bathroom door open it bumped up against my Mothers foot. She was lying left side on the floor. Blood was everywhere. I ran the warm water and began to clean her up. She was out, so I started with her legs first. I was not ready to hear the moaning, so I was waiting until last to wash her face.

My Brother was at the door with the towels and I took two from him and gave one wet towel to him and one to my Sister. We knew the routine. My Brother and Sister began to clean the walls, the dresser and the floors. I had washed off my Mother's arms and the bathroom when she began to come to. I began to wash her face and she looked up at me and said with a bloody mouth. "I got him this time!" I shook my head like I did not know what she was talking about. She reached behind the trash can and pulled out her rose from Smokey Robinson. "See!" I started laughing...to this day I don't know why but Mom started laughing too. She stood up and began to wash her own face. It was like the Smokey Rose had given her this new power , this new strength. She pulled out Dad's wallet too. She had stolen it from him, and he thought he had lost it at the concert.

We walked down the street to the McDonalds which was open late, and we got cheeseburgers and fries. We laughed and ate and enjoyed our orange sodas. Mom told us not to tell Dad. We didn't and when he returned the next afternoon we acted like nothing had happened. Mom planted his wallet underneath the seat, and he found it later that evening. He didn't remember how much money he had, and it was then that she discovered he never kept track of his money. She would use that to her advantage.

CALIFORNIA

After the Smokey Robinson concert my Dad decided we were too broke to stay in California. Or maybe he was threatened by Smokey. Once we returned home my Nanna began to visit more often.

Besides being very intelligent Women my Nanna informed us that we were "born with a veil". Apparently, some people are born with a veil, caul, or hood, over their face. According to my Nanna, being born with a veil is a sign of special destiny and psychic abilities, or good luck.

For the record, google quotes a similar definition.

My Nanna was notorious for showing up at our house before the "final blow". She would call first and if she could not reach our home she would have one of her church friends bring her to our home. I do not know how she knew, but she just did.

She was a Godly Woman and something about her presence made my Dad stop. A lot of times he would cry after she left. She always forgave him and for the times that she prayed for him. Our house would be a place of peace for at least a couple of weeks.

There were times when my Dad was choking my Mom and as soon as her eyes would roll up in her head my Nanna would knock on the door.

There was a time when he was punching her so hard she stopped talking and again at 3 am my Nanna showed up at the door.

There was a time he hit my Mom's head on the bathtub, and he was just about to stomp her in the head when my Nanna called out my Father's name. He froze mid-stomp.

She saved my Mother's life often and I could not understand why or how she knew and why God always brought her to our home right in the nick of time.

One Saturday night after church I asked her, "Nanna, how do you know when to come over our house and keep my Mom from dying?"

She smiled down at me, "My heart, all the Women in this family were born with a veil. We can feel and see things. Your Mom and your Grandma don't really tune into theirs, but I believe you are in tune to yours. You do the same thing, like knowing when to get up and check on me in the middle of the night."

"Nanna, that's scary. I don't want to be in tune. I want to be tuned out." She stood up and walked off laughing. "Girl, you tickle me."

I lay back on the bed and prayed. "God, please tune me out." But He didn't.

SOMETHING WEIRD

The next evening my stomach hurt. I told my Nanna that something weird was going to happen and that's when she began to pray.

It was Saturday and we were about to sit down to watch Soul Train when my Aunt Drenay asked my Mom, "Did you ever cry over Mike?" My Mom looked at me and shook her head no. "Well, you know kids process death differently than we do."

My Aunt Drenay stood by my Mom through thick and thin. She would fight my Father if she was around during one of my Mother's beatings. She would do everything she could to keep him from hitting my Mom She was the youngest girl in my Father's family but the roughest. She would yell at my Father and tell him he was wrong whenever she saw my Mom hurt...and sometimes she too would cry. Often she would come over to the house and try to sit there waiting out my Father's temper. It seemed my Father did not want to hit my Mom when my Aunt Drenay was around.

I woke up to seeing the Jacksons on Soul Train. Aunt Drenay was jumping up and down looking out the front door. It was my Uncle Jahawn. Aunt Drenay had always had a crush on my Uncle Jahawn and although he paid her no mind he was a gentleman with it. "Heyyyy Jahawn!" Uncle Jahawn smiled and nodded his head. He had taken his hat off before he spoke to her, "Hello Drenay, how are you today." His voice was deep and strong. He stood tall over everyone. "Hello, hello." He spoke to everyone in the room. My Grandmommy came out of the kitchen. "Hello handsome!" Everyone loved him because he was a gentleman. Handsome like a light skinned Billy Dee Williams. "Hello Mom." He knew how she had treated my Mother, but he was respectful, nonetheless. He looked down at me, "Come on Princess I came to take you over to your Great Grandmother's." I smiled and jumped up into his arms. "Girl, you are heavy!" **That was the first time he used that sentence; the second time was the day he rescued us from Foster care.**

FOSTER CARE

We were sent to Foster Care several different times and each time I would just wait it out. I knew we would eventually return to our home. I would constantly pray about my Brother and Sister and pray that no one was hurting them. When we would reunite we would tell the stories of our Foster Mothers and then laugh at our experiences. We were always glad to be back home...with each other.

My Foster Mothers were always black and generally went to one of the churches where the members knew of our family or knew members of our family. Whenever we went to visit whatever Baptist or Adventist church with our Foster parents someone would ask..."Isn't that Fleta and Charles' daughter?"

My Great Grandmother Johnnie knew most of the church community and always made arrangements for the Foster parents to bring us to her home. We would stay with her until the day we had to go back to the Foster parents' home and put our show on for social services. As soon as social services left, the Foster parents would take us back over to our Great Grandmother's.

We had a caring and loving church community. They were a group of people who made sure we had clothing, food and care, particularly when we were taken from our parents. It was strange but we actually looked forward to foster care.

We would smile sometimes when we went because everybody knew the game. Police picked us up... conversation with a social worker. We were sent to some home...the person would know our Great Grandmother and give her a call. She would have them bring us over or would arrange to come get us.

She would let the foster parents keep all the money. Virtually, with no responsibilities. She just wanted to make sure that the three of us always landed in her home and felt love and knew our family. She wanted us to know that we had family that was there for us. When my Half Brothers and Half Sister were staying with us, she would keep them as well.

My Uncle Evan and my Uncle Wade were the main ones my Nanna called to come and get us. I think they thought we were just hanging out with all of her church friends, but they always made us feel loved when they picked us up. I would laugh at them when my five-foot two Great Grandmother would tell them what to do or would fuss at them. They would just look down at me and say..."That's your Great Grandmother." She may have gotten on their nerves, but they stayed respectful. I learned that from them. How to respect your elders. I learned from these Uncles...my Mother's Brothers...the things a young girl should look for in a man.

I suppose the most memorable house I was ever taken to during the "foster years" was the very first one. When I arrived at the house I thought it was like in the picture books. A white picket fence and stairs that led up to the front door. There were chairs and a swing on the front porch. As I walked up the stairs with the social worker I saw lace curtains in the windows. This was probably a church woman...yep, probably. The social worker rang the doorbell. I looked up at her..."Where are my Brother and Sister?" She shushed me.

An older lady opened the door. She was probably in her late sixties, very proper. Her hair was parted down the middle, she reminded me of the pictures I had seen of Rosa

Parks. Her hair braided down on each side. She was wearing a gray house dress with stockings.

Her house smelled like antiques and she spoke eloquently and quietly.

She and the social worker were having a conversation, whispering and every so often the older lady would glance over at me.

The social worker approached me, "Ok, so I am going back to the office..." I interrupted her..."Where are my Brother and Sister?" She opened the door, "You will be fine here for a while until the court figures out..." I interrupted her again..."Where are my Brother and Sister?" She looked at me and walked out the door. The older lady who was to be known as Ms. Yarbrough motioned me to the living room.

She pulled out a piece of paper, sat next to me and began to read the rules of the household. She read quietly and matter of factly. I wasn't paying attention. I was only focused on how I could get out of her house to find my Brother and Sister.

Ms. Yarbrough asked my name, "What is your name, girl?" I looked her in the eye, and I asked, "Where are my Brother and Sister?" She didn't smile, only sighed. "Ok girl,

Foster Care

well let me take you to your room. The room was gray like her dress. It was a temporary room. White bed like the hospitals and hotel soaps with a washcloth on the dresser. The floor was white tile. There were no pictures on the wall and the window fashioned bars.

I already hated the room. She told me there were clothes for me in the drawers and books for me to read on the shelves. She informed me that in the morning I would walk to school with a friend but for today I would eat in my room and read, and tomorrow I would walk to school with another child. She asked if I had any questions. I said, "Yes, where are my Brother and Sister?" She didn't answer. She closed the door and locked it.

I lay on the bed trying to figure out what to do. I got on my knees. "God protect my Brother and Sister. I don't care what you do to me and if I need to be a sacrifice so that they are ok...please do that too." I refused to cry...if I did that I would be weak...I had to be strong so God could do what he was going to do and I had to continue to pray that he would take care of my Brother and Sister.

I woke up the next morning to her standing over me. "It's time to wake up, girl. Wash up and come down for breakfast. Your clothes are on the dresser." The clothes were nice. An expensive dress and some black and white saddle shoes...longer than my knees of course. Round collar and a sweater. I washed up and put on the clothes. They smelled good.

When I walked downstairs I could smell the bacon. It smelled good and I was hungry. There was another girl at the table my age. "Hello," she said as she put a piece of pancake in her mouth. I said, "Hello." I was served a pancake, a piece of bacon and some eggs by Ms. Yarbrough. I said, "Thank you." Ms. Yarbrough smiled, "Well it is good that you have manners." When Sara came to me, she didn't have any." She looked at the girl across from me. Sara nodded. "You will walk back and forth to school today with Sara...understand?"

"Yes ma'am." I responded. Ms. Yarbrough laughed, and her big stomach bounced. "Girl, who taught you those good manners?" I said, "My Nannah". "Your Nannah?" "Yes, ma'am that's what I call her. Her name is Johnnie Lucille." Ms. Yarbrough leaned back with her eyes wide open, "Johnnie? Is your Nannah? An usher at the Seventh Day Adventist Church?" "Yes, ma'am she is." "I know her...Oh my LORD! Ok girls...well go on and go to school. I will see you when you get home."

Foster Care

She pushed us out the door and I kept looking back at her. She was standing in the window her hand over her mouth.

Sara started talking, "You should get used to this because it is going to be your home." I rebutted, "No it's not…I have to find my Brother and Sister." Sara kept trying to convince me, "I thought the same thing, but I never saw my Brother and Sisters again, but I am ok. You and I could be Sisters. We could talk about girl stuff and I could tell you about boys that like me, and I bet when you get to school, boys will think you are cute too. You have long hair like mine"……Sara continued to ramble. I tuned her out. I remember introducing myself as the new girl in every class and trying to stay to myself during recess and lunch. I didn't like anybody, and I didn't want to get to know anybody. I wasn't going to be here long and so I didn't want to make any friends.

I walked home to Sara's lets-be-sisters diatribe and began again to focus on how to get out of this house so I could find my Brother and Sister. As we walked home I saw the 8th Street bridge. I knew how to get to my Grandmommy's house from there. I had walked many times with my cousin Dennis to the ditch from her house. We would go to the river to throw rocks.

When we walked in Ms. Yarbrough sent Sara to her room. She told me to come to the dining room. When I walked in My Nanna was sitting at the table. I ran to her and began crying! She held me close and said, "My sweet baby. God works in mysterious ways." Ms. Yarbrough was crying also. She bent down and kissed me on the forehead. "You have no idea the love your Great Grandmother has shown me and my family."

My Nannah looked at me and said, "Ok love, we are going to keep a secret, me, you and Ms. Yarbrough. Ok?" I nodded, "Yes Maam." You are going to stay with me this weekend and then come back to Ms. Yarbrough on Monday morning. Ok?" "Yes maam". "We are not going to say anything to anyone about this. Ok". "Yes maam".

When it became dark, we slipped out the back of the house where Ms. Gonzales was waiting for us in her car. I was instructed to lay down in the back of the car and my Nannah threw a blanket over me. Ms. Gonzales said, "Hello, Miha". I said, "Hello, Ms. Gonzales."

Foster Care

My Nannah was in the front and as I fell asleep I heard snippets of their conversation. "It's so sad". "I know honey but that's my Great Granddaughter and I will die and go to hell before I let this happen." I was to find out later that Nannah had a huge network of friends. She was blessed to find out any and everything...even when she wasn't looking for it. I was to find out later that she would pass that gift on to me.

The next morning, I woke up in my Nannah's house and she was sitting right next to me. "Nannah can you help me find New and Mel?" "Already on it love." She winked at me. I have a friend in social services, and she found them last night." I hugged my Nannah. Well let's get up and eat some breakfast, we are about to have a great day." I could not quite understand what was going to be so great about it.

About an hour later, the doorbell rang. I heard a lady say, "Girl, it was a trip, but God is good. You got them until August...whew girl you owe me!" They both hugged and laughed out loud. I could not see them, but I could hear them. "Nanna, do you have any food? We're hungry!" It was my Brother and Sister! I ran to the living room and they both screamed my name. "Yvonne!" I hugged and kissed my Brother and Sister. I walked them to the table and started fixing them plates of food. My Nanna walked in..."No ma'am! Here you get to be a little girl. Go ahead and sit down and let Nanna do that. I am sure you all have adventures to share," She gave me her matter of fact face.

I looked at her through tears..."I love you." Later that night, as we slept in the same bed with my Nanna I thanked God. "God you did it, and fast. I love you so much and thank you for making sure we are all ok. Now could you please watch over my Mom and if it is your will please kill my Dad."

We not only stayed with Nanna during "foster times" but we also stayed with her on the weekends. I don't know how she did it, but she would feed us and clothe us, and she always had enough. She knew how to make things from the Goodwill look good and she would share how to accessorize and how to keep our clothing clean. We learned how to wash clothes with a scrub board and how to treat collars and the underarms of clothing. She taught us how to use the old tub washing machine with a ringer and she would sing gospel songs as we turned the crank outside in the backyard. She taught me how to wash clothing and underwear by hand. She knew I had to take care of my Brothers and Sisters so she made sure I knew but she told me to "teach them how to do it when they get old enough" so that they will know how to do it for themselves.

She told me that I had to learn how to live through the tough times and she would say "As long as there is some kind of soap in the house you can keep yourself and your clothes clean." I did teach my Brothers and Sisters how to wash their own clothes and sometimes we laugh about the times we have had to wash our clothes by hand. For me this was an act of love passed down to me and from me to my Brothers and Sisters, and then to my Daughters. I remember smiling when on different occasions my Daughters stated, " Mom I was on the college struggle bus, so I had to wash my clothes by hand." We would giggle together, but we were never ashamed. We felt more blessed about having a tradition of endurance.

My favorite part of housework was always when Nannah was ironing. It was when she would tell her stories. She would be ironing shirts for mostly white folks in the community. The white men would come and pay her to iron their shirts. They most of the time paid her double for the work. One white man smiled at me and said, " Your Nanna does a better job than the dry cleaners. She is amazing. My shirts are always white and starched to perfection. The dry cleaners turned my stuff yellow and I thought 'I will never do that again'!" He kissed her on the cheek as he left. He paid her three times his usual that day.

Nanna would iron all of her clothes for the week and then all of our clothes. Sometimes she would tell my Mom to bring "all" of our clothes and she would take them to the Laundry mat and wash and iron all of them. She never liked that my Mom would throw all the clothes into one machine all together. Nanna believed in washing whites with whites and colors with their individual colors. "When you mix up clothes like that the clothes look dingy. There is no reason for black folks to make themselves look any poorer. Even if the clothes are not new, washing them the right way can make them seem so." Then she would kiss me on the forehead.

Most of the stories she told while she was ironing were about her grandkids...she would lean way back in a high pitch laugh and say..."LAWWWD those kids were bad!" Generally, she would start with the boys and then end the night with talking about my Mom and her Sisters.

THE STORY

Tonight, I asked her, "Nanna, tell us about the story when Mom and Uncle Josh hid in the grass. She chuckled and slapped her knee. "Well your Grandma had cleaned up Katelyn and put her in a cute little white dress. I could never understand why your Grandma would dress her up for her to go outside and play. Anyway, she yelled to your Mom and Joseph to keep an eye on their little Sister. I believe Katelyn was about three or so. Well, they said Ok Mom, but kind of half paid attention. Katelyn was on the porch at first but then she got up and started toward your Mom and Josh.

I was watching from my house, which you know they used to live right next door? I nodded. Well your Mom and Josh had found a tire, probably from a 19-wheeler or something. This street is so busy with highway traffic I could not believe my Daughter would even let her kids play out there like that. Anyhow, I stood at my screen door to make sure they were ok.

Right about the time Katelyn got to the edge of the road her Brother and Sister were running towards her with the semi-tire. They had that tire moving real fast with the sticks they had, and they were running right next to it. Right at the time Katelyn turned to her left she was knocked down by the tire. Just like something you would see on that roadrunner cartoon. I put my hand over my mouth, but I could hardly hold in my laugh when I saw Katelyn get up with the tire marks up her whole body even on her face"...she laughed a hearty shrilled laugh. Boy, that tickled me. Katelyn didn't cry or anything, but she went to the house and in about five seconds your Grandma came out screaming for your Momma and Josh. I could see them. They were right in front of my house hiding in the grass, but the grass was so high your Grandma couldn't see them. It tickled me that they were right in front of her face and she couldn't see them. After she went back in the house they both stood up and started laughing.

I yelled at them, "Hey you two!" They looked scared with their eyes all bugged out. "Get in here before you get a whippin'!" They came in and I started them making cookies. At dark, your Grandma came to fetch them and asked them where they had been. They both sang, " We were at

The Story

Nanny's." I just smiled at your Grandma, but of course she just rolled her eyes and took them home." She slapped her knee and started laughing again…"Boy that just tickles me." She walked into the kitchen and I smiled to myself thinking about how cool it must have been to live next door to Nanna.

RETURN TO THE WAR ZONE

On Sunday, Mom picked us up as usual. She had a big knot over her eye. My Nanna sat her down on the couch and began to pray for her. My Mom did not want to pray. She was angry, but she ended up sitting on the couch and crying. My Nanna sent us to her room; and we sat in there looking at books, listening to my Mother cry while my Nanna consoled her.

I sat down at the vanity table and looked at all of my Nanna's perfume's. They were in all of these pretty colored bottles. Different shapes and sizes. There were perfume spray bottles with blue stuff, purple stuff and green stuff in them. I looked at myself in the mirror. I began talking to myself, " You are a beautiful black girl and when you get older no Man will ever hit you. Not going to happen, you will not stand for it. You are going to know your Bible and you are going to marry a Pastor, but you gotta learn your bible."

Return to the War Zone

My Brother chimed in, "Yvonne you don't need to know your Bible, you just need to make sure you have hats and gloves to match your clothes, Stupid!" "What do you know, Hickety Head?! You don't know anything about being in the church, because you always fall asleep in church." My Sister was laughing. We both looked at her, "What is wrong with you?" She snickered, "Hickety Head". We all started laughing.

"Come on!" My Mom walked in and motioned us to come out of the room. "I have already been here too long." My Nanna's phone rang. It was my Father. My Nanna gave my Mother the phone. "I'm sorry, we are leaving now." She gave the phone back to my Nanna. She was crying violently. I knew my Father had threatened her and I knew what he would do when we got home. My Nanna waived us off but stayed on the phone with my Father. As we walked out the door I heard Nanna say, " I want to pray for you, don't let the devil use you, not tonight...."

We went to the car and we were silent. Usually my Mom would ask us about the weekend, but she just kept crying and looking at us through the rear-view mirror. I wondered what she was thinking.

Charismatic Violence

There were days when we would come home from Nanna's and things would be fine. There were days when we knew Nanna had gotten to him because his eyes were red. That meant he had cried to her about something, but she always kept his secrets. She would never tell us what they shared. She kept his confidences. Then there were the other times. The times when he would meet Mom at the door with his fists. The blows always sent her reeling. He would beat her for the times he forgot to beat her. He would make up things to beat her for. Then he would go through her purse. He knew Nanna would sometimes give her money so he would take the money and go out with one of his girlfriends and not come home or he would just take her money and leave and not come back for a few days.

My Mother and my Nanna had come up with a plan for that. My Nanna would tell my Mother to leave five dollars in her purse but take the other forty dollars or whatever extra she had and put it in her sock in her tennis shoes. This way it would not fall out if he hit her and if he ripped her clothes off he would not find it.

Even if he thought five dollars was all she had he would take it and leave. Most of the time he had taken her money, so she would not eat all weekend; but after he would leave

Return to the War Zone

Momma would walk us to 7 Eleven and buy us some bread and some bologna. She would fix the sandwiches for us on the side of the store and tell us we had to eat it then. The Black man in the 7-Eleven would give her packages of mustard to put on the sandwiches and sometimes he would open a bag of chips and tell my Mother that the chips were going to be thrown away anyway.

We would put the chips in our sandwiches and eat it all at once. We thought it tasted good. My Mother would eat with us and we would laugh and talk about silly stuff in the dark. The black man would give us soda sometimes too.

Most times we would come back home and go to bed. Since my Father was gone for the night we slept well. A few times we saw his car parked in front of the house, so that meant I would have to hide the meat and bread in my coat or my sweater. In the summer, I would put the bread and meat outside my window and then when it was bedtime I would open up my window and put the food in my closet. Then I would get a big cup of ice from the kitchen and take it to my room like I was eating it. I would put the meat package in the cup on top of the ice to keep it until morning.

My Father thought he was starving us on those nights, and he would even make a plate for himself and give us a speech on why we didn't deserve anything. He would even brag about giving "our" money to his women. He would say in front of my Mother and in front of us the things he was doing to those women and the things they were doing to him. He would keep talking until one of us cried so we took turns being the "one who would cry". Me and my Mother that is. My Mother learned very quickly not to say, "The kids shouldn't hear that" because it resulted in a severe beating for her.

He would sometimes pull out pictures of his women and put them in my face. He would tell me how much of a whore my Mother was and that she was not a virgin when he married her and that I was going to be a slut just like her. He said we were not going to amount to anything, that we were going to be useless and that he knew it. He would brag about his side girlfriends all the time and then about three or four months after speaking about how he was leaving us for them he would come back to my Mom crying, saying he wanted his family.

I remember wishing he would actually leave us for someone, anyone.

SURPRISE SIBLINGS

I was sitting on the floor coloring and watching Soul Train. My Brother and Sister were on the couch watching right along with me. The curtains were open, and the sun was shining through the house. It was a beautiful morning in Colorado. Mom had been cleaning the house all morning and was finishing up in the kitchen. She was yelling at us after every song played on Soul Train, "Who sings that? Who is that song by?" We would laugh because Momma wasn't really the music mogul person in the family, but it seemed that we always knew the musicians. In that way, we were our Father's children.

We did not know where Dad was, but we were ok with that. It was right before the Soul Train line came on that he walked in. He held the screen door open for a moment and looked in to see who was in the living room. It was almost like he was scoping out the place. He looked down at me sitting on the floor. "Yvonne, come here." I walked over to the front door and looked on the porch to see three young kids standing on the stairs. Dad slammed the screen door in all of our faces. "These are your Brothers and Sisters." The kids looked at me like they wanted to be liked.

Dad had walked through the kitchen and was heading down the stairs .

I opened the screen door and said, " Hi guys, do you want to play?" They smiled and moved very quickly to come in the house. When they walked in they were greeted with smiles from my Brother and Sister. "Come sit and watch Soul Train with us!!" My baby Sister hit the couch with her hands. "Okay!!" they sang in unison.

We were all watching Soul Train for a minute when my Mom walked in the living room. I held my breath, wondering what she was going to say, wondering what she was going to do. She smiled at them, and said, "Come here babies!" She hugged on them and kissed on them. "Welcome to our family! Well, now things are going to be even. Three boys and three girls how cool!" She then turned and went in the kitchen.

I walked in the kitchen a bit after her and looked at her. "Mom did you know about them?"

"No." She whispered. I could tell she was hurt. She lifted my chin with her hands and looked me in the eyes. "It is not their fault. They are just kids and who knows what is going on with their Mom, but it is ok. I believe all kids need love so that is what I am going to give them."

And that is exactly what she did. Our new siblings went everywhere with us; family vacations, school and even over to Nanna's for the weekend. I do not know how Nanna fed all six of us, but she did.

It would be that our Brothers and Sisters would be in and out of our lives from their date of entry and into adulthood. We would bond with them and then their Mother would take them from us. She would transition them every six months to a year. She would get tired of them and drop them off at our house and then six months to a year later, she would show up unannounced to take them. Each time my Mom would yell at her and beg her to let the kids stay. My Mother wanted them to have a stable home, if that is what you want to call it.

They also experienced seeing my Mom get beat up and they were just as scared as we were. We were to find out that their Mom had experienced beatings as well. Only she took it out on them. When my Mother was beaten they would all hide and cry. We would wait until my Father left and I would clean her up and the mess like always; but only now the newbies would come and help. I remember saying, " No, no, no... I don't want you guys to get in trouble." But they would say, "So what, we are not going to let you do this by yourself."

My Father was still harder on the boys and we would see them get beat a lot. As Sisters, we were always figuring out how to nurse and bandage our Brothers' wounds. After a while, the boys would compare wounds and make jokes about them. We became very close and determined that if there was ever going to be a fight with one of us, it would end up being a fight with all of us. When we were together we looked out for each other, we covered for each other and we lied for each other. We did anything we could to protect each other.

Unfortunately, they experienced the same wrath that we did. They were referred to as "those kids" by my Dad's family or even described as "the extra kids". Whenever they were attacked, just like I would do for my full blood Brother and Sister, I would step in front of them. Even to the point of enduring spankings. They were "my" Brothers and Sisters and nobody but God was allowed to judge them or hurt them. It was frustrating to be on constant guard, but as I grew up I replaced the frustration with Anger.

BEING ANGRY

Throughout my life we would go to my Great Grandmother's on the weekends and by the time I was in junior high, I was angry. I was angry because I was not getting regular sleep; I was angry because I did not receive any gifts at Christmas; I was angry because I was taking care of five children I did not have, and sometime s eight; and I was angry because I was a teenager.

My Father was still throwing my Mom into my room in the middle of the night. She would be covered with blood and I was still cleaning it up. One night I was truly pissed off and I decided to "show him". I would lock my door and he would be able to bring her into my room. I locked the door with my teenaged mind set, feeling like I was going to be the winner. It took a couple of nights, but sure enough he threw her against the door. It didn't open. I heard him try to twist the door open but to his surprise the door would not budge. I sat up in my bed looking at the door. I smiled to myself and took a deep breath.

I had won. They would not be bringing their crap into my room, ever again. I lay down on my pillow expecting to fall asleep. It was quiet, with the exception of some whimpering I heard just outside the door. Then all of a sudden I heard a scream that sent a chill through the floor to my spine. He was trying to bust down the door...with HER!! She was screaming from pain and he did not stop until he successfully got her head to go through the middle of my door. She was passed out. When he reached over her head to open the door her body slid with the door into my room. Her back was to me and blood ran down both the front and back of the door. I was sure she was dead.

My Father was breathing heavy. He was staring at me with red eyes and since he was light skinned his skin was red. He almost growled at me, "See there, YOU almost got your Mom killed. Lock the door again and I promise you I will kill her." I got out of my bed and I just stood there staring back at him. I was just as angry! I had decided at that moment that I wasn't going to back down from him. I was THAT teenager that didn't care...at that moment...at that very moment I knew what I could do to hurt him back. All of these years, I had been the audience for the show he wanted me to see; but I knew that he loved me and THIS time I didn't care about his feelings. I only cared that HE had crashed through MY door! I clinched my fist and I looked at him with the same eyes he was looking at me and I said in my deepest voice, "With everything I have I HATE YOU!!!"

At that very moment I saw my Father's heart. The angry face subsided and he began to cry. It was as if he had been stabbed in the heart. He slicked his hair down and put his face in his hands and began to cry. I stood there looking at him and my Mother's body with her head still in the door and I remember thinking. "THIS crap, this mess...will NEVER be me! No man will ever beat me! Ever! Not without suffering the ramifications!"

My Father walked out of my room crying and went downstairs to his room where I could hear him wailing. I walked over to my Mother and gently took her head out of my door. She fell back into my arms. "Mom?" She jumped and then I jumped, "Yes baby?" My voice was like a defibrillator to her. She must have felt she had to live, at that very moment, for me. I grabbed a pillow from my bed and propped her head on it. I stretched her body out on the floor.

I headed to the bathroom but first stopped in my Sisters' room to see if they were ok. They were on the bed holding each other and crying. I went to their room and wiped their tears. "It's ok. I got it. You do not have to worry about it tonight ok? I love you." They whispered, "We love you too, Sister." I pulled the cover over them and kissed them both on the cheek.

I stopped in my Brothers' room. They were all three looking at me with big owl eyes. "Everything is ok you guys, so you can go to sleep now." They all let out deep breaths . I covered them as well. "Listen boys, I am your big sister and you know that, right?" "Yes, they all answered in their prepubescent boy voices. "Ok, then you know I will die before I let someone hurt you right?" "Yes Sister." I smiled at them. "Ok, I love you". "Love you too Sister." I kissed them all on the forehead.

I closed the door softly and proceeded to the bathroom. I could still hear my Father whimpering as I warmed a rag to clean up my Mother. When I walked into my room my Mom had turned on to her side. Her hair was stuck to her head with blood. I took the warm rag and began to wipe her face and clean her hair. It would be seven trips later that I would have her all cleaned up. I put a blanket over her and then lay on my bed to go to sleep. The last thing I remember hearing was my hamster running on his wheel.

FOR WHATEVER REASON

"Yvonne get your ass up out of the bed!" My Father came in the room the next morning and he and my Mom were standing at the foot of the bed. My Father was holding my Mother's hand. "You were disrespectful last night, and I don't appreciate it and your Mom doesn't appreciate it either! We talked about your smart-ass mouth and we decided together that you are grounded for the next two weeks. You don't get to go no damn where! Right baby?!" He looked at my Mother and she nodded her head. "Now you can just stay in your room!" I was still being belligerent, so I asked with an attitude, "What about school?" "Of course, you will go to school!" He slammed my door.

I thought to myself, Are you friggin kiddin me?!! What the f?!! I got ready for school and left without saying goodbye to anyone or eating breakfast. I hated my life!

I was bigger than everyone at school especially the boys; so, anytime I had an opportunity to beat them up, I would.

Charismatic Violence

Eddie was my favorite target. He was feeble, but stupid. He liked me and so I hated him because that is what you do in fifth grade. Eddie would bring me candy and I would beat him up. Eddie would give me a flower and I would beat him up. Eddie would write me a poem and I would beat him up. Eddie would never hit me back because he was not allowed to hit girls, but he would beat up any boy who tried to "like" me.

I landed in detention all the time, but I kept good grades to keep my Dad off my back. This particular time, my teacher said that because of my detention numbers my grades were going to start suffering. She was a big lady with glasses and when she notified me of this consequence I shrugged my shoulders and said, "SO!" She grabbed me by my shoulders and shook me until I began to cry. I ran out of the room and to my house. When I got home my Mother, face bruised and all, asked me what happened. I told her about the teacher shaking me; and my Mother promptly went up to the school and shook the teacher in front of me.

The teacher ran out of the room to the principal's office and brought the principal back to the classroom. After my mom threatened to sue the school, the principal asked my Mother to withdraw me and take me to another school. My

Mother said she would "love nothing better." My Mother signed me out of that school and promptly slapped the principal before we left.

In the car, my Mother was cussing up a storm as she expressed how nobody had ever better mess with her Children. I was staring at my Mother with my mouth open. Who was THIS WOMAN and where had she been all my life??!! When Momma got home she told my Father about the situation and together they were hatching a plan to make sure "NOBODY" ever messed with their kids. I hugged them both and told them thank you and they said things like "We love you baby, yeah, you belong to us and we will kill somebody over our kids...all of ya'll". My Dad called us all into the living room. For the next four hours we listened to my Father talk about how he would kill for his kids and how he would hurt anyone who messed with my Mother or his family. He talked a little about his childhood and then went back to us and comparing himself to tigers and roaring lions when it came to defending his kids.

He finally let us go to bed at 2 am and he and my Mom went to their room laughing. For whatever reason, we were a tight family again.

Charismatic Violence

I walked up to my hamster Tarzan's cage. He stopped running on his wheel and walked up to the bars. "Tarzan. What just happened? I am so confused by today." Tarzan lifted his nose up. I opened the cage and put him on my shoulder. He sat there as I got my pajamas. I put him on the bed, and he sniffed around while I changed into my pajamas. I picked him up again and kissed him on top of his head.

When I got in the bed and lay on the pillow he scampered up the covers to my neck. That was where he slept when I let him out of his cage. I felt him snuggle into my neck and I fell asleep. Tonight, everyone could sleep in peace.

FIGHTING

It was Friday after school and I couldn't wait to get home. We would be packing to go over to Nanna's. Mom grabbed our bag and we kissed Dad goodbye for the weekend. When we arrived, Nanna came running out of her house, as usual. Her arms were always open for hugs. She gave us so much love. Her high-pitched laugh always made us giggle. My Mother told us to go into the house. I sat by the screen door so I could hear.

It was my Mother, "Well she has been getting in trouble, fighting and going to detention. I don't know what is wrong with her." My Nanna said, "Well, I am going to speak to her about it, but YOU know what is wrong. She is living what she sees." My Mother said, "Well, I don't need a speech from you right now and..." My Nanna cut her off, "You don't need a speech, but you are going to get one...hold on...Yvonne get out from behind that screen and take your Brother and Sister into my room." How did she know I was there? "Yes ma'am."

Charismatic Violence

I grabbed my Brother and Sister by the arm and went into my Nanna's room.

When she came into the house she called out to me and my Brother and Sister to come into the living room. She had us sit on the floor in front of her. "Babies, I want to share something with you that happened to our family, ok?" We nodded. She pulled off her shoes and put a pillow on her lap. She rubbed the pillow as she began...

My Great Great Aunt was about eight months pregnant. She was drop-dead gorgeous. Chocolate skin and that hair like your Mother's, curly, long and wavy. She was married; but Men still tried to talk to her, even though they knew she was married AND pregnant. But I remember when she became pregnant she was even more beautiful. We nicknamed her exotic because she looked like she had American Indian, Black and African in her. She was striking. When she smiled, it was like she sent out radar to Men and they would just swoon around her, no matter the race or color, or whatever. She never cheated, though...she loved her Husband to the end.

They say that is why she was always glowing. Because she was in 'true' love. You know, they say that when a Woman is in true love that she glows. They also say that

Fighting

"Babies made from two people in love are generally the most beautiful babies. So, don't have any babies by someone you don't love... because then you might have a bugaboo." She giggled.

Well, anyway, this particular day my Great Aunty was walking home from work and she decided to go the "pretty way" by the railroad tracks where you could see the river afar off. She liked it because it was quiet, and the railroad tracks reminded her of her walks and talks with her Father. There were butterflies everywhere and it always smelled like fresh cut grass. Her Father had walked with her that way many times when she was a girl. They had admired the wildflowers.

On this day she was listening to the water rustle under the wind to her left and enjoyed the smell like fresh cut grass. She took a deep breath and smiled. Her tummy moved and she began to rub her belly, "Oh you like that smell too? I knew you would. I can't wait to meet you." She watched her stomach moving and she took each step on the railroad track. The baby in her stomach was making her feel amazing. This thing called pregnancy had made her feel like a true child of God and she had told everybody that. The baby kicked again. "Oh, you must be hungry. We will be home soon." She just knew it was a girl. There was just "something" that made her know it was so. The baby began to kick and with every step it kicked harder. "Oh my, what's going on in there? Whatcha tryin' ta tell me. We will be home soon love." The kicks got harder and more frequent.

She was just barely at the beginning of her eighth month, so for certain this was not labor. It was the last hard kick that caused Aunty to fall to one knee and when she did, that is when she saw him. The man standing at the edge of the trees. He was smiling...his blonde dirty hair blowing in his face and mouth. "What you doing out her gal?! You know this ain't a free passing lane for your kind?" She began to walk faster. He was walking behind her. Yelling out stuff that she did not comprehend.

Her instincts told her to run. She was running when a truck with other Men in it who looked like the tree man pulled right in front of her. She fell down but got up and tried to run around the truck but one of the men jumped down from the truck and grabbed her. "Gal you gon' have to give us something so you can pass through this here train track. Whatcha got that you can give us?" She shivered, " I don't have anything, I don't have any money, but I know how to cook and clean. I could come by in the morning and clean up your house. I am a Woman of my word and I will do what I say." The Men laughed, "Naw, our wives wouldn't like that now would they?" She looked at the ground, "No I guess they wouldn't."

Tree man had caught up to them, "The only thing I see is that baby, my wife can't have no babies, but she sure would like one she could play with every once in a while." My Aunty stood with her head down. Tree man continued, "I got this paper here that says that you sign over all your rights to that baby to me and my wife and we will raise it. We will make sure it has a good place in the barn to sleep and my wife can be happy."

He put the paper and a pen in front of my Aunty's face. She began to raise her head slowly and she placed her hands to her sides like a military shoulder. She rose her head and looked up to the sky. "We are ready, Lord." She walked past Tree man like he would actually let her walk home. "Girl sign these papers!" She kept walking. One of them picked up a rock and threw it at the back of her head. When it landed she grabbed the light pole next to the track to pull herself up. The baby was kicking. She whispered, " I know Evan Clarence, but it will be over in a while". She felt another rock hit her back and then the pelting became more frequent. She held onto the pole with her back to the offenders. She continued to whisper to Evan Clarence, "Hold on now, pretty soon you will get to see Mommy. I am already proud of you." She felt warmth running down her leg and she knew her water had broken. The ground, at first, just went but then became red.

She could not hear Tree man and his Brothers anymore, but she knew they were close, and they were still throwing rocks. She felt the blood cake her hair and running down her face. Suddenly her feet were in the air. She could see the river really clear now, the sun glistening on the water. She knew her body was jerking and though she was choking she saw Tree man through the blood in her eyes. He was walking up to her with a knife. When he stuck the knife in her stomach she screamed but could not figure out where all that air had come from. She was determined to stay alive long enough to see her son.

Treeman was laughing..."Ho, look at this one, he would a been a good worker on the farm!" She was still alive...blinking, looking, trying to see her son. Treeman lifted the baby up in the air. "BEHOLD!!" Treeman was laughing now holding the baby up for her to see. She saw her son and to her he was the most beautiful thing she had ever seen. With her last breath she said, "Evan Clarence, let's go home."

Folks say that after she lay her chin on her chest lightening came from a clear sky and struck one of Tree Mans Brothers dead. Treeman dropped the baby and they all ran and jumped in the truck and drove away.

My Aunty hung from that train pole for three days. People in the passing trains wondered what in the world was going on where a dead woman was hung from a train pole with a baby attached to her by an umbilical cord. They looked out the window as if it could not possibly be true."

My Nanna turned to me, "We decided as a family that we would never ever be uneducated to where we are broke and cannot pay to get our family taken care of. Your Great Aunty hung there for three days because we did not have the intelligence nor the money to get her down. Oh, we tried; but the Sheriff and the coroner were working together, and THEY decided that until we paid a fee we would not be able to take down the body. Eventually, we were able to pay and get her down, but we decided as a family that this would never happen again.

Charismatic Violence

So, young Lady, I ask you, "What will your legacy be?! You have an obligation to do well in school, to represent your family with class and to speak like you have some sense. You WILL conduct yourself as a Lady and you WILL educate yourself and your family EACH and EVERY time you have an opportunity. Do you understand?!" "Yes ma'am". You will stand and fight for what is right, and don't you ever let anyone mentally beat you! You have an obligation to make sure that the woman who hung on that train pole did not die in vain."

That night I dreamt of my Great Great Aunty. I was not sure what she looked like, but I am sure it was her. I was walking down a train track and all of a sudden she was right behind me. When I turned around it was like her spirit went through me like a wind and she said, "YOU are me."

NEW ATTITUDE

When I hit eighth grade I was on the honor roll! I had been for two years straight now and I was winning awards for perfect attendance and good grades. I worked hard and anytime I became tired I would remember my commitment to my legacy, to my Nanna, to my parents and to my family.

In high school, I remember being a part of many groups and from ninth grade wondering how I could get into Howard University. I had heard of famous Black people graduating from Howard, like Roberta Flack, Phylicia Rashad and Toni Morrison. I wanted to go to Howard because I had heard it was like the Black Harvard. I felt like Howard would give me this Black pride and Strength that I was not getting here in Colorado. It was not that my teachers did not try in Colorado it just seemed their resources were limited.

I was at Central High school in 9th grade when my parents decided to move out to Littleton. The house was a beautiful house with a plush crème carpet throughout and we were certain that we were going to be happy. There was plenty of room and our rooms were downstairs, spacious and right off the bar. We were definitely going to live the high life here. The first few weeks were a tornado of getting registered for school and unpacking.

The first day I went to register at Littleton High School I was actually excited. The school was huge and looked so clean. It smelled like a place where learning was taking place and I could not wait to see the library. When I walked in the building with my Mom some of the students stopped walking and began to stare at us. They were whispering and some of them had frowns on their faces. I was surprised. What was happening?

When we went in the office the front desk ladies and the other front office staff were genuinely kind. They were welcoming and after a series of signed papers the front office lady with the bun stated she would take me to class. "Have a great day at school baby." I looked back at her with a scared face. The halls were clear now and the bun lady was giving me a tour. The library was amazing! I could not wait to check out some books. The gym was great, as well as the rest of the campus. When we landed at my room door, the bun lady said,

New Attitude

"Wait here." She went in and came out with a very staunch looking June Cleaver look-alike.

June went into the class and I heard some scuffling which sounded like chairs were being moved. June came to the door and motioned me in. The class stared at me as I walked in and there was not one smile. June escorted me to the back, right corner of the class. "Class...continue to read chapter four like I said." All heads moved down as if to pray. "You can sit here, Yvonne. I figured you would like it here by the window. That way when you can't keep up with us, you can just look out the window." I looked up at her quickly. I squinted my eyes at her.

As I watched her walk back to the front of the room, I remembered what my Nanna had said, "The best way to get back at people who are idiots is to do well!" I was about to get A's in her class, and she didn't even know it.

The first few months I performed well in all of my classes. My grades reflected it and June Cleaver made sure to keep the compliments to herself. June, however, was never without a comment. When she gave me an A++ she said in my ear, "How will this help you be somebody's maid?" Another time she whispered, " Welfare recipients do not generally care about getting good grades...hmmm surprising."

What she didn't know was that my creative writing teacher was pushing me. Excited about my stories and my writing. She had a staunch face, but she would come to my desk with this passion in her voice. " Yvonne...Oh my! Now this is worth reading!! Amazing!" She would hug me and say, "Where do you want to go to college?" I laughed, "Are you serious? My parents are not going to be able to afford that. Ms. Staunch, I am just trying to survive!" I walked out of her class frustrated. Why does she keep doing this? I am just going to get out of that crazy house and work as many jobs as I need to so I can survive. STUPID!

The next morning after June had told me that most people my color end up fat and unattractive. I was grabbed by the arm by Ms. Staunch. I looked up at her not understanding what was going on.

"We are going to the office right now young lady". My mouth was open, but I thought it best to keep my comments to myself. Ms. Staunch whisked me in the room with the school counselor. There were College pamphlets on the table. The counselor began, "Yvonne, based on your grades you can get into either one of these schools. We also pulled some black schools for you just in case you don't like white people."

New Attitude

The two teachers smiled at each other. I looked at both of them, "It's not that I don't like WHITE people, it's just that I don't like PEOPLE white, or not, who think that I am stupid and that I am incapable of THINKING! I picked up the Howard University, Clark Atlanta University and Bethune...hmmmm. How amazing would it be to be surrounded by my own people. I knew there were black thinkers out there, my age, I just had to find them. Ms. Staunch, grabbed up a couple of Junior College pamphlets and one for University of Denver, University of Colorado and Colorado State University. I was thinking, Whatever!

She grabbed a piece of paper and wrote down the black college pamphlets I had picked up. She hurried out of the room but yelled over her shoulder, "Hurry up so you are not late to my class."

At lunch, I found a spot way out in the field to sit down on the grass. I pulled out the pamphlets from my backpack and began to read through them. The black kids in the pamphlets looked happy. They were wearing nice clothes and they were hanging out with each other. I gasped and whispered to myself, "Is that a black professor?"

After I read every word of the three pamphlets I began to cry. Something came up and out of my spirit, but it broke me down. I began talking to myself, "Man up! You know what this life is! No trippin and no weakness and don't be stupid. No dreams!"

I walked to the trash can and deposited the pamphlets in the trash can. The lunch bell rang.

Two weeks later I came home from school and my Mother was in a super great mood. What was this all about? She hugged me and kissed me when I came in the door. Huh?

I had just finished changing when she burst through the door. "Guess what you got in the mail today?! Look!!"

There were envelopes, letters, flyers from colleges. Mom was jumping up and down. "I am so excited for you!! I didn't even know you wanted to go to college! You would be the first one you know...wow...this is crazy! I love it and I love you!" She slammed the door behind her.

I sat down with all the mail and began to read the letters. "Hello Yvonne, we are looking forward to talking to you......would love to have you come for a visit...please call the following number to schedule a visit."

The envelopes contained catalogs with pictures. I kept the black college ones and the one from University of Denver. I took the books apart and began to put the pictures of the students on campus on my wall. I thought, How would I do this, how could I do this? Wait, why does this say I am on their mailing list. How did I get on anyone's...? Aw hell! Ms. Staunch.

My Mother was humming and singing that night while fixing dinner. When my Father came in he was actually in a good mood. He called all of us out of our rooms and gave us kisses on the cheek. He even kissed my Mom on the lips and hugged her. He told her how beautiful she was and that he had the best family in the world.

We were not quiet at the table that night, we were laughing. I was laughing at my Little Brother who was opening his mouth with food in it, trying to make my Sister throw up. My Mother and Father were eating in the living room, like always. They had their trays in front of them and they were watching TV, as they ate. Dad was talking about the guys at his job and how they were getting on his nerves. My Mother, of course, was mostly silent nodding her head in agreement.

My Brother, Sister and I were laughing in the kitchen, now talking about the kids who had gotten in trouble for sleeping in church last weekend. We were in the middle of a deep laugh when a tray came flying into the kitchen and subsequently my Mother.

My Father came in shortly after and landed three punches to her face. 'What the f--- are you talking about her going to college for? You are a dumb b----! I didn't go to college and I am fine! Are you trying to call me stupid?!" My Mother shook her head no. My Dad stomped over and stood in front of me. He put both of his hands on his waist, "Are you trying to go to college?" I looked at the floor, "No sir." He was panting," Then why in the hell is that bull---- coming to the house in your name?" I kept looking at the floor, " My teacher Ms. Staunch put my name on the list, I think." "Hmm she does not have any right to do any s --- like that. She's an idiot! You ain't going to college, you gonna be a whore slut like your Mom! Well, I'll fix all that...hmmm...college!!" My Mom made her way to the bathroom dripping blood I was going to have to clean up. She was moaning from pain.

My Dad called the three of us into the living room and told us to sit on the couch. We listened to him yell about not having clothes and shoes stapled together and taking a paper bag to school with grease in it for about 5 hours. He was not done until two in the morning.

New Attitude

Once he was done he made us give him a kiss goodnight and then he went to bed.

We waited to see if he was going to hit my Mom again, but all we heard was the sound of the bed creaking. It was often he would have sex with my Mother after beating her.

The next day when I came home from school he told me to come downstairs. On the bar were all kinds of drugs and paraphernalia.

He said, "Sit down, I want to show you what this is all about." He started off with showing me what he called "Christmas Trees" then he progressed to windowpane, heroine and finally marijuana. He showed me how to roll a joint and told me that one day I was going to get high with him and my mom so they could see what I was like when I was high.

The whole time he was talking I was in a different world. I remember thinking, "This is the most idiotic crap, who teaches their kids about drugs? Seriously you think teaching me how to roll a joint is critical to my development? That's stupid, that's stupid and THAT is REALLY STUPID! Only idiots like being out of control of their faculties. Are you serious...ok so this is the DAD that I have...God I am not sure why, but OK!!

Once my daily drug lesson was over I could go to my room. What an idiot, he took up my time for the unnecessary. I put my books on my bed and looked at Tarzan. He was holding on to the bars looking at me. I smiled at him, "I know Tarzan, I think it was a stupid waste of time too!"

I was to get my "drug" lesson daily. I was certain there would be some drug dealers' education certificate that I would receive at some point.

During my days at school, I would hang with Robert and Kate. Robert was a six-foot-tall man with what he called at the time, "very feminine ways". I knew Robert was gay, but he knew that he would not be accepted at Littleton High School. Kate was about four foot one with big breasts and a huge back side. She had huge front teeth which were crooked and rotten. I was of course, tall and skinny with no curves at all. We were a motley crew.

After my first day at school, a girl named Terrie walked up to me in her cheerleading outfit and said, "Aren't you on the wrong side of town?" I looked right back at her, "Excuse me?" "We don't want your kind at this school...just so you know. YOU are not welcome here." I looked back at her, "I hate it here anyway!"

As she walked away, Kate walked up and said, "Come with me, they hate me too. I am for sure an outcast and SHE well, SHE is the most popular girl in school. Her dad owns some furniture warehouse or something. She thinks because she has money she can treat people like crap."

That day I learned about the have and the have nots from Kate. People would bump into us and throw stuff at us and often they would just pour water over her head or squeeze mustard in her hair. She would just act pissed off and head to the bathroom to clean herself up. Robert would sometimes stand up for us but would get pushed down and be promptly called a fag, but he would fight again if he had to.

We tolerated the bullying for a while but made a pact to always walk to school and from school together. It was the first time I had ever been in the unpopular crowd. Kate's mom was married to a war veteran and every so often he would pick us up from school. He always wore his old military jacket, tattered as it was, because he would relapse into thinking he was on a mission.

One day he picked us up and he immediately jumped out of the car and screamed, "Hurry up, hurry up, hurry up! I have people after me. They are following me in black cars." Kate giggled, "Here we go." We all jumped in and instead of heading toward Robert's house he took off on Colorado Boulevard. Robert scrunched down in the seat, "This is bullshit!" It made both me and Kate laugh. "DUCK DOWN!", the veteran motioned his hand to the back. We ducked down in the seat. I started laughing really hard and nudged KATE. I was looking at Robert. "Look at apple boy." Robert was livid. He was tired and wanted to go straight home. About ten minutes later, The Veteran did a u turn and informed us he had lost his stalkers.

He looked through the rearview mirror, "Do you kids want some ice cream?" Kate said, "Sure." The Veteran stopped at Baskin Robbins and we all had a good laugh about it. Kate explained that she was used to it and for the most part just remained calm until the episode from her Stepfather was over. She told us that there were many nights the Veteran would just get up at 2 am throw his army jacket on over his pajamas and speed off in the car. He always came back and had "accomplished his mission".

New Attitude

The Veteran came back and gave us our ice cream cones. "Kate here tells me that you all are being bullied?" We all nodded. "Hmmm...we need to address that situation now, over. I will figure something out, but for the rest of the day I have to stand down. My covert operations need to be quiet for tonight. Bullies huh?"

We all sat quiet and ate our ice cream cones. Robert was dropped off first, then me. I was always grateful for a ride. I walked at least 10 blocks home and 10 blocks to school every day. Most of the parents gave their kids rides to school or the kids had their own cars. My parents made it very clear they were not going to drive me. Even when it snowed. Generally, on snow days I could count on Kate and the veteran to be waiting on me around the corner. I would get in the car, "Thank you so much! I really appreciate this." The Veteran would nod at me sitting in the back, "You know, I am on assignment to protect you, over. I don't know who assigned me, but I know I am on it." I shivered, "Thank you." Kate turned back and smiled at me, "You're welcome love."

One day in the cafeteria one of the football players decided he was going to squirt mustard all over me and Kate and Robert. He was squirting the mustard from the jar and holding it at his groin. He thought it was funny and so did half the cafeteria. I was pissed.

When he began to walk away I picked up a chair and hit him as hard as I could on his legs. He fell to the ground but when he turned to look up I had his head between the legs of the chair. "If you bother me or my friends again I am going to seriously hurt you!" He looked scared. Robert pointed his finger at them, "Yeah!" Kate was giggling like she always did. For the next few days people moved out of our way at school. I am certain they thought I was crazy. We loved every minute of it.

On Friday the Veteran picked us up and as we pulled off Kate pointed to the guy who had squirted mustard on us. The Veteran sped up and pulled the car over. "You guys stay here, I got something to do!" He gets out of the car and goes to the trunk. When the trunk closed we saw what looked like a military issue machine gun and The Veteran walking towards the football player.

He never pointed the gun at the football player, but we heard the conversation. "See that burgundy Ford over there?" "Yeah." "You mean yes sir, dontcha son?" "Yes sir". He lifted the gun and pointed to the car we were in. "Do you see those people in the back of that burgundy car?" "Yes sir."

New Attitude

"OK good, well take a good look at them three because I have been ordered to serve and protect those three. Understand?!" He was in the football players face. "Yes sir." "Ok good because if anyone lays a hand on those three over there YOUR head is going to spray paint this cement. You got that!?" The football player nodded through tears. The Veteran walked back to the car and put the machine gun in the trunk.

"Fake gun gets him all the time! Pansy!" We had a new respect for The Veteran after that day. We would even participate or create a covert mission on occasion.

Life at school after that was pretty dull. No bullying to run from. We were still the outcasts, but at least now we were the safe outcasts.

One cold day, I headed out the door for school and Kate and The Veteran were not there. I knew the drill, that meant that I had to walk to school. It was cold that day and I remember seeing the yellow Caprice, but the snow was blowing in my face, so I ignored it. I trudged along and did my time at Littleton High School. After school the last of the snow had landed in its final resting place. I walked home humming a Stevie Wonder song (as around the sun the earth knows she's revolving and the...) The yellow Caprice pulled up. A twenty something looking guy rolled down his window. He was kind of cute. His hair was brown Beatles style and he reminded me of Davy from the show The Monkees. "Hey, can you tell me where the grocery store is?" He smiled. I yelled from the middle of the street, "Yeah, you have to go back to Colorado Blvd up that way!" I pointed behind me. He pulled off. I continued to walk and convinced myself that I liked the crunchy sound of my boots in the snow. I wasn't looking up until I reached the corner.

The Yellow Caprice pulled up right in front of me. The twenty something had his pants pulled down to his knees and he was stroking his personal. I screamed. He smiled. He liked that I was afraid. I took off running down the street in the direction that forced him to have to drive in reverse. He was laughing out loud and I was running as fast as I could in the snow in my boots. Two black men came out of an apartment and I ran straight to them. I told them that a white man was chasing me with his penis out in that yellow car.

The Black men took off running, but twenty something now driving forward and sliding in the snow hit the gas. When he turned right, the black men almost caught the car but fell in the snow trying to open the door. I heard one of them yell "Damn....did you see that?!" The other one was bent over breathing heavy from running. "Yeah Man". They walked back over to me. "Are you ok?" I shook my head no and started crying. One of the men went back into the apartment building and soon the police appeared. I gave a description and both men gave an account of their story. The police offered to take me home.

When we arrived at the house my Dad walked outside and asked the police "What happened?" They explained the story and my Dad looked down at me. It was a strange look, confused, angry and passive at the same time. When the police left, my Dad grabbed his jacket and slammed the door to go outside. He didn't come back until one in the morning.

I could hear him and my Mother talking in the living room and I was to see a scene I could not believe. My Mother was holding my Father in her arms and my Dad was weeping. He kept saying, "I couldn't protect her, I didn't protect her." My Mother kept rocking back and forth with him saying "It's ok."

Early in the morning, my Father opened my door so hard it hit the wall. I jumped up in my bed. "Hey, how much do you like your friends?" I wiped my eyes, "I only have two friends, but I hate this school and I hate this neighborhood.

Last week that Terri girl told me that they "don't allow black girls to be cheerleaders here". My Dad said, "Hmmph, well there it is then."

Two weeks later my Father came to the school. He interrupted the creative writing class and told me to "come here." I was headed for the door when my teacher said, "We are in the middle of class, is there...?" My Father interrupted, "NO there isn't, I just took her out of this school since we are moving." Ms. Staunch was frantic. "What?!" "Yep!" My Father looked at the class, "and by the way... there's no college sh - - happening here!" The students were laughing. I grabbed my things but before I reached the end of the aisle, Ms. Staunch grabbed my face and lifted my eyes to hers. "You are an amazing Black Woman and some day you will write or say or speak something that will change lives. I...love you and everything that YOU are going to be!"

I believed her.

SCHOOL DAYS

Most school days we would wake up to three bowls, cereal and milk, already on the table. That meant they had made up the night before and she was trying to get back in the bed with him to keep him happy. This would last for weeks sometimes; but on the days when we woke up and she was cooking in the kitchen. we knew on those days that things would take a drastic turn.

I could not wait for Mondays because it meant I could go to school! I would thank God for School. School was part of the world I felt I could control. It was my escape from all of the drama at home. It was the place I could pretend nothing was wrong. I had many friends, many flirts and many people who wondered..."how does she do it?" I was in fact in everything I could be in. Honor Society, peer counseling, cheerleading, Future Homemakers of America. My club memberships and activities ran the gamut. Anything I could do to rationalize leaving the house. We had moved to an area by a place called Ruby Hill. We didn't know our neighbors, but they would wave, and they wouldn't stare.

I was going to South High School now and I enjoyed everything that was going on. My principle was Black and respected. My friends were Black, White, Asian, Mexican, Spanish, druggies, Nerds, Honor students, bikers, athletes and whomever else I could befriend. South fostered so much cohesion it was almost like its own developing melting pot. The students stood for what was "right" and we didn't care what color or click you were in. If you were down for the cause, that was all we cared about.

The first day my Mother and I pulled up to South High School I saw that it was a big school and it scared me. I looked at her and said, "Mom?" She kissed me on the forehead and said, "It's going to be ok, come on." All I could do at that moment was remember my "big, other school" experience. This school was huge and had a bell tower. I was going to be depressed, I just knew it.

When we got to the front door my Mother looked back and took my hand. "Come on, I am scared too, but I am going to be with you all the way." When we walked in the doors, there were students everywhere. Of course, the bell had rung. God was punishing me. As we walked in a couple of guys stopped and said, "Well Hello!!" One particular

School Days

gentleman said, "They call me Flex." He was pushing his friends back and out of the way. They were all shaking my hand and a few of them kissed my hand. I was confused. I didn't know what to do. Guys had never paid attention to me like this before. In fact, they had only called me over to play football once, when I was in sixth grade. Because they thought I was a boy.

 A kind lady with a blonde beehive motioned for the boys to get out of the way. She said, "I'm so sorry about that. You know young boys and testosterone?" She and my mom giggled as she ushered us into the office. My Mom was filling out paperwork and I watched the many colors and orientations of people walk in and out of the office. The office staff was of different colors and varieties also and they all seemed very happy. I was given a hall pass from Ms. Beehive. "Mr. Maxey, will you take this young lady to her first class?" A handsome young man turned around and said, "Yeah sure". He was just a little taller than me, but his chest and shoulders looked like the hulk. He reached for my hand but before he could grab me, another hand pulled me away. "Naw, I will escort her." A cute young lady winked at me. She pulled me out the door before he could respond. "Welcome to South, I will be your friend, ok?" How was I to know that this wonderful woman was to be my friend for over 40 years.

SOUTH HIGH SCHOOL

I had been at South for one full year now and pretty much I had one best friend. We were to confide in each other, and I was to find out that she lived with abuse on a daily basis, as well. The only difference was she was the one being abused. "Hey girl!" I walked over and gave her a hug. "What's up?" She smiled but flinched a little as she pulled away. "Sindra, what happened?" She looked at the floor…"She beat me with the iron last night." I interrupted…."What?!!! What the fu…?"

She burst out…"Apparently, she did not like the makeup I was wearing…" "She is crazy as hell! Well what did your Brother do when he got home? Girl he didn't know…How could he not know if you"……. "My Mom made me stay in the closet all night and when she threw me in there she told me if I said anything she would choke me to death with the iron cord…girl she had that cord in her hand and was looking at me like she was gonna do it too!" "Sin that is a trip!"

South High School

Two guys from our senior class looked over at us..."Hey beautiful and beautiful two. We both sang..."Heeey." We knew how to turn on the charm and turn off the pain. "Ya'll going to the Sadie Hawkins dance?" Sindra giggled, "We don't know yet?" Why do teenage girls always answer for each other? We grabbed each other and laughed as the boys walked away. The Sadie Hawkins dance was a dance in which the girls were supposed to ask the boys. Sindra wrapped her arms in mine..."Girl, Delaren just wants you to ask his floodin' butt to the dance..." "Girl I know," I whispered. "But why is he always flooding?" We both laughed out loud as we walked into class. I would not be asking Delaren...I would be going with Reggie...my boyfriend who attended another high school.

My teacher walked up and hugged me. "Yvonne, I don't know how you do it. Once again, you aced the assignment." I smiled as she handed me my paper. I thought about my Great Auntie and whispered, "This one is for you." I was never going to be like my parents. Never!!

In school, I liked winning. I liked being the best reader or having the best attendance. I never missed school, if at all possible. In fact, I would go to the nurse's office and sleep for a period, if I was sick, rather than staying home. I would get perfect attendance awards all the time and tried to keep myself involved in everything to avoid being at home.

I had been quiet with my achievements in elementary. I was always the new girl because my parents were consistently getting evicted. So, I did well with my homework, and I read everything I could get my hands on. I remember Beverly Cleary being one of my favorite authors and then asking the Librarians what I could read next. I remember asking one white Librarian how come there were no books about Black people. She said, "Well, that is a good question?" I was always in the library during my open hours. It was quiet, peaceful and I could escape to another world. One day, she walked up to me and she said, "Hey, here is a book by a Black woman, maybe this will be good. It was "The Bluest Eye" by Zora Neale Hurston. I loved it and I began to read her work.

I loved everything about her work. The accents, the tone and everything that came with being Black. I was reading about people like me and I thought it was cool. I had begun to read about strong women, and I became intrigued by women who I thought were strong, such as Eleanor Roosevelt, Jackie Kennedy, Coretta Scott King. I would watch shows with and fall in love with women who I pictured I could be. There were Thelma on Good Times, Cleopatra Brown and Cecily Tyson because she was a dark Black Woman on television. I thought in silence what it would be like to be like these women, but I kept that to myself and navigated quietly through the halls... but that was about to change.

MRS. BETTE COX

Ms. Cox reminded me of my Great Grandmother, only she was white. She dressed extremely well and always smelled good. I was in Ms. Cox's home economics class when she approached me one day about being a class officer. "Not interested." The bell rang so I picked up my books and walked out of the class. The next day, Ms. Cox told the class that we would need to elect officers and we should think about nominating someone in class who always completed "her" work and that we could depend on. No one said anything. At the end of class, Mrs. Cox placed a candidate form on my desk. When I walked out of the class that candidate form was still on my desk.

When I came into Mrs. Cox's class the next day she had created ballots. My name was on the ballot and I raised my hand. "Uh, Mrs. Cox, I said I didn't want to do this. So, can you please have everyone scratch off my name." "Absolutely not." She said it so matter of fact. "Ok everyone, let's vote."

Mrs. Bette cox

One of the three guys in the home ec class leaned over, "Yvonne you would actually be a great class President."

"SHUT...UP". I rolled my eyes at him. Once the ballots were filled out, Mrs. Cox placed the names and number of votes on the board. I had won and I was livid! People were saying congratulations and I was HOT!

When the bell rang, I grabbed my books and was prepared to storm out after the rest of the students when Mrs. Cox stepped in front of me. I was sure she was going to apologize or tell me how she messed up; or even try to explain with humility how she wanted me to try something new. But Mrs. Cox stood in front of me and placed a packet on top of my books. Very nonchalantly, she said, " This is your leader's guide, make sure you read it and be prepared to conduct our first meeting on Friday." I rolled my eyes, but she didn't get to see it because she walked confidently away from me and down the hall.

Ms. Bette Cox had a way of making students achieve, even when they didn't want to.

She knew I was hiding something at home because sometimes she would send me to the nurse's office to sleep. One day she asked me what was going on at home. I looked up at her..."nothing, why?" There is blood all over your hands. I hadn't remembered to wash them. How could I have done that? It was dark when I had left the house to catch the bus for drill team. How stupid! I looked at my hands covered in dried blood. "Oh, I cut myself and I thought I had gotten all of it." She sat down next to me, "Yvonne, there are..." The bell rang, and I grabbed my stuff and left. We both had tears in our eyes.

Ms. Cox invited my parents to school to talk to them about a program she wanted me to be involved in. This particular week was not so bad for my Mom, so she was able to wrap her head in a scarf. She looked cute in her scarves. The whole drive to school, my Father complained. He hated dealing with teachers, this was a waste of his time; and of course, if he "finds out I did something crazy, I was going to get my ass whooped".

My Mom whispered, "She is a good student." My Dad slapped her. "What!? What's that you say?! I will beat you right here in front of this school." Mom was trying to hold in tears and took out her powder case.

When we walked in Ms. Cox had everything on her desk. She had us all sit down at the table and began to discuss the FHA office, the next level and an organization called Delta

Mrs. Bette cox

Epsilon Chi. She was going to have me run for a regional office and then a state office. My Dad was already complaining about the cost. Ms. Cox assured him there was no cost and that there were plenty of funds within the organization. My Dad got up, "Well, it's whatever she wants to do! I'll be in the car!" He pushed a chair out of the way and left the classroom.

Ms. Cox acted like what he did wasn't important. "Ms. York, thank you for your support, I believe Yvonne will do well." My Mother stood up nervously, "Ok, thank you so much." Ms. Cox grabbed my Mother's hand and whispered, "Here is my number and there are resources out there to help you. You and Yvonne can stay with me...I..." My Mom cut her off, "I have three children and sometimes six ! Are you prepared for that?! No! I didn't think so!?"

Ms. Cox was tearing up and so was I. She hugged me before we left. On the way home, Dad slapped Mom into the window several times. He blamed her for letting me read. He was yelling about how I was not going to be anything when I grew up...what was the point! he yelled. The next morning, he knocked on my door. When I opened it he said, "We didn't get to do this kind of stuff when I was young." His eyes were watering, and he was talking so that he wouldn't cry. "I'm proud of you. Your Mom always says you were a mistake…but I never thought that…never thought that…never will."

He hugged me and walked out of the house. I came out of the room to see my Mom standing in the hallway. I didn't know she was there. She smiled at me and walked into the kitchen.

REGGIE

When I met Reggie, I was in junior high. I was a loner and seemingly always angry. On the first day of junior high all the guys in my class walked up to me and asked me if I wanted to play football at lunch. I thought that was cool that the boys liked me and said, "Yes!"

At lunchtime, Reggie walked up to me and said, "Okay, you're on our team." I took off my jacket like the rest of the group and laid it on the grass. Reggie's eyes opened wide..."Oh shit". I jumped..."What!"

"We thought you were a boy! You're a girl?!" I was devastated! I went home and told my Mom and it seemed she was aloof. It almost seemed like she was happy that I was feeling persecuted. She had this smirk on her face. I remember thinking, "What kind of Mother does this?" One day I came home, and my Mother had bought me a pair of those silky black pants that everybody was wearing. She told me she bought black because I could wear them with different shirts. She had bought me one of those MaDrenay cut up like shirts and it was fitted. She had bought me a new bra and panties. She had even bought me a bra with a little pad in it. I needed the padding...really needed the padding. A couple of the shirts had some bright red in the patterns and so my Mom bought me a pair of bright red tennis shoes. The next day I put on my outfit and my Mom said I looked sexy.

I had never felt sexy. She had even braided my hair back on one side. I walked to school that way with pride. I am sure I got there right at the bell so that everyone could see me walk up. A couple of the guys were like..."Whoa is that the same girl from yesterday?" A white skinny guy with his hair like Paul McCartney when he was a Beatle said, "Hey I'm Bill". He was cute. "Hi Bill," I said. He said, "I like what you are wearin.'" Then he walked away. The girls standing next to me said, "That is one fine white boy."

We were in the sixth grade and I had no idea I wouldn't kiss him until late in the seventh grade. I felt sexy all day. The guys were grabbing my hand as I walked by giving me compliments. I felt like I was MaDrenay sexy that day. My Mom had done it. She knew what to do to make me feel special. When I came home I fell into her arms crying. I told

Reggie

her she was the best Mom ever! My Mom said to me, "It was always in you, Vonnie, we just needed to bring it out."

I called myself secretly seeing a guy during school, nicknamed Buzzy. He was nice enough. He was muscular and kind. He would bring me stuffed animals and hearts. I liked him a lot. He was in Golden Gloves Boxing and when he won he brought the trophy to school and gave it to me. In front of everyone. He kissed me and I really liked the way he kissed except he had really bad breath. I didn't know how to tell him, but I was prepared to love him anyway.

Everyone who knew me knew my policy on sex. In fact, I had bragged about it in school. I had said that I was not going to lose my virginity until I had graduated from high school...and that is what I did. However, this particular day all of our friends had decided to walk across the street to the local burger joint located across from our junior high school. Buzzy asked me what I wanted, and I said I just wanted some fries. The fries were about 57 cents. I hugged him after he bought the fries. I thought that was so kind of him. Then he asked me the question. We were holding hands and he looked into my eyes and said, "Von, when do you think we can hook up?" I said, "What do you mean?" He said, "When are you going to give me some?" I was enraged, "SEX!" He looked at our friends because they were staring at us. He muttered, "Well...yeah." I started digging through my purse for change. He asked me what are you doing? "I took out nickels, dimes and pennies from my purse and threw them at him. "Fifty-seven cents! Really! You think that what I have is worth fifty-seven cents!! Go to hell!" I stomped away and I could hear our friends laughing behind me.

The next day Buzzy came to school with a cast on his fist. His friend came to my locker and said, "Ay, Buzzy was so hurt by you breaking up with him yesterday that he punched the bark of a tree. He went to the hospital last night and they put the cast on his hand." I said, "Well that was stupid!" I looked across the hall at him and rolled my eyes...although my heart felt bad for him...but I didn't want to be vulnerable. Plus, he thought I was only worth fifty-seven cents. I was done with him. It was two days later that Reggie approached me at my locker and said, "I know we been best friends for a long time, but I would like for you to be my girlfriend. I won't mind waiting either. I will wait for you forever."

The words sounded so wonderful to me. I told him, "I don't want to mess up our friendship, Reggie. Can you give me a couple of days to think about it?" He said he would and that began the first time I would find true sacrificial love. A

Reggie

week later Reggie approached me and said, "Look if you don't want to be my Girlfriend then just say so!" Don't have me waiting all day!" I liked that about him. To me, that proved he was strong. I knew I would need a strong man to stand up to my Father. Reggie would prove to be a ride or die boyfriend.

THE BUS

My Father would never ever get up and take me to school. Even when it was blistering cold. He said he did not want to start doing something he could not finish. No matter how high the snow. One time I asked my Father to take me to school and he yelled at me all the way to school, to the point I started crying. I never asked him again. I was always late catching the bus to school. Most times I was late from lack of sleep. Having to stay up to listen to my Father's rantings and ravings or him beating up my Mother.

The bus driver would see me and wait for me, as I would run across the field and get on the bus. I would always ask myself why I was always late. Why it seemed that I could not get there on time. Truth is I am still that way on occasion, but not as much as when I was young.

I would go to school and do well. Join and start groups, stay on honor roll, and most quarters had great attendance. I never wanted to stay home...even when I was sick.

The Bus

I had told Reggie yes to his proposal and he immediately was the epitome of a man. He was on my side, right or wrong. If I was in an argument with someone, he would get involved and come at them if he saw them. When I told him about the things my Father had done to my family, his face was angry, but he didn't cry. He took me in his arms and said, "I will take care of you, don't worry." He was to in the future show me what a caring, loving man was like. He was the one who came over; and for some reason, my Father was afraid of him. My Dad tried to control our time together. Whenever he got mad, now he would always beat my Mom and my Brother, but would come in my room and say, "You can't call Reggie for two weeks or he can't come over here for a month. You're going to be a whore just like your Mom was. Did you know your Mom slept with a whole bunch of guys in high school? Yep, they told me about her. I was just the dummy who married her because she was pregnant with you. You were a mistake, but my Dad told me to make her an honest Woman and be a man! I wasn't ready to marry her, and I didn't want to marry her! You are going to be a whore!"

When I would start to cry, my Mom would come in the room behind him. For some reason she would risk herself by defending me. She would do things to turn his attention to her. This day, like others, she did it again. "Charles, she is not a whore!" He whirled around, "What?!!" "She is not a whore; she is still a virgin. She is and that is what she told me, and I believe her!" I peeked around my Dad to look at her. She winked at me through the yelling. She smiled at me and I smiled back. I felt her Motherly spirit radiating from her. After she smiled, he slapped her to the floor. She began to scream his name like always. He was crashing her into the table and smashing her against the wall. He was choking her. She had saved me the only way she knew how. She was protecting her children from his fists, taking his hits, blow by blow. Gasping for air, as he choked her. I stood there watching him this time. I didn't close my door. Sometimes if he saw me crying, standing there he would stop.

He threw her to the floor, and she slid to my feet. I looked down at her and then slowly up at him. I was crying and I whispered, "Please stop." He looked at me and turned his head sideways like a curious dog. He grabbed his keys, his coat and all the money out of my Mother's purse and left. My Mom smiled up at me through bloody hair and face. Before she passed out, she whispered, "You are not, nor will you ever be, a whore."

The Bus

Reggie and I continued to date, even though my Father told me to stop seeing him. He would send me letters or wait to talk to me at school. When it was cold, his Sister would wait a block away and then they would give me a ride to school, so I wouldn't be cold.

My parents were not stable, so I went to three high schools. I landed at South and I remember my Father saying, " Ain't no guy going to still date you living way across town." He was wrong. Reggie would take three buses to come and see me and later, I, him.

When I was taken into custody by the police when my Dad punched me in the eye, Reggie called the police. He thought my Dad had killed me and hidden the body. He said the police told him, "She is in protective custody.". Reggie told the police, "I need to see her or talk to her and let her know that I am looking for her…that I love her." The officer told him…"Look man you are under 18 and I can't help you. You're not family!" Reggie said he went back and got his Sisters and they came down to the police station with him. The officer wouldn't budge. Reggie said he "prayed and prayed" that God would bring me back to him and then a week later…He did.

Charismatic Violence

When I finally talked to Reggie, I explained that my Father had blacked my eye and the school had removed me from my home. I told him that my Aunt Katelyn had come to get me, and I was now living with her. Reggie immediately got on the bus and said it would take him about two hours to get from Aurora to Littleton, but he would be there.

When he arrived, I cried in his arms for at least two hours. He held me and reassured me he would always be there for me, no matter what. "First, we are going to go to Howard...make something of ourselves. No coming back here. One day I am going to take you away from all of this. You deserve better, a better life and I love you." I laid my head on his chest and said, "I love you too."

QUIET INTERRUPTED

It was pretty quiet this night. I listened to my stereo as I did my homework...Lionel Ritchie was singing "Sail On," which was appropriate because I was feeling my vibe tonight and sailing through my homework! I was a straight A student...I was going to be somebody...I knew it. My hamster Tarzan was feeling his vibe also. He was running on the wheel and it seemed to spin to the music. Tarzan liked music almost as much as I did. My room was clean, so I let Tarzan out for a while so he could run around the room while I put my books away. The DJ was playing late night love songs and something by Kashif was playing...It reminded me of Reggie...but then so did everything. I picked up Tarzan to his dismay...kissed him on the head and put him back in his cage. He went straight to the corner of the cage...he knew what time it was...he began rustling and building a circle around his butt to get ready for bed. I plugged in the nightlight and turned off the room light.

I laid in bed and thought about the day. School had been awesome; Reggie had brought me candy out of the blue. Troy was back in school and told me that he loved me and thought about me while he was in juvenile...what the hell?! I had ignored Troy and walked away. I had received all my tests back and of course they were all A's. I drifted off to sleep to the sound of Stephanie Mills singing..."I feel good all over..."

"I heard my mom scream "Charles!!" as she came flying through my door. He had picked her up and thrown her, not expecting the door to fly open. She was crying and bleeding on my carpet...I was thinking...NO! Not tonight! She started crawling. I looked up at my Dad. His hair was messed up and it seemed like the conked hair stood up on two areas of his head...like two horns...like the devil...his face was brick red and his chest was heaving...he stared at me...distant and angry...I was scared.

He picked her up off of my floor by her throat and said to me..."Don't you move...lay down and go back to sleep." My mom was choking in the air...he kept her lifted in the air as he walked out with her dangling and slammed my door. I heard him throw her to the ground. I did not cry anymore but I was pissed at them for messing up my perfect night! I was trying to make myself feel something for her, but I couldn't.

I had been able to tell when they were headed my way. I would hear the car door slam and knew that they had been drinking and doing coke, or windowpane, or acid or something. This time I heard him say…"You think I'm playing with you?" She was sniffling. She didn't really scream anymore, but you could hear things crash when he threw her. She would now only whisper…"Please, please, stop, please"…he never heard her. They were in the hallway now right by my room. I began to get ready…I moved the covers from my legs and put my feet quietly on the floor…careful not to creak the wood…He was calling her bitch and slut and she was grunting as he punched her in the stomach…okay now one knee on the floor and second knee on the floor…he was yelling at her right outside my door…turn to the bed and put your hands together. The door flew open as he kicked her into my room…Pray!

I heard him standing behind me…I could feel his breath…hear his chest raising up and down…I could smell him right behind me…could feel him just standing behind me staring at me…waiting for me to be scared, so he could pounce on me…but I would not stop praying…don't stop praying...nothing can beat God...kept on praying....nothing can beat God...keep praying...nothing can beat God!

He left her sobbing in my room...I heard him grab the keys. My Mother was muttering again...the car sped out of the driveway...he would not be back tonight. I thanked God for sending his son Jesus down to stand between me and my Dad. God always worked...always!

WHY WHISPER?

She sometimes was allowed to walk in the house. Most times he threw her in. Usually she was drunk and on some sort of hallucinogenic. I heard him yell something out of the car and speed away. I got out of my bed and knew she would mumble and walk around outside for at least five minutes. I ran to my little sister's room and gently picked her up. I walked as fast as my seven-year-old legs would carry me…I had to make sure my sister was safely in my bed.

My little brother was asleep in my bed already….always in the fetal position. I slipped my Sister under the cover next to my brother. I had started to protect them from my parents.

I went back to my Sister's room and arranged the pillows in the bed under the covers so it would look like my Sister was asleep in her own bed. Sometimes my Mom would go into my Sister's room and lay next to her and babble. My Sister would cry because she was scared and the next day I usually had to wash the covers and sheets of my Mother's blood and then I would have to wash the blood off my Sister. My Sister...with blood dried and caked in her hair. I would wash it out and we wouldn't discuss it; but when it was all out, I would tell my Sister how beautiful her black hair was and what a wonderful little girl she was. My Sister had the most beautiful little deer eyes and would look to me for approval. I assured her she was beautiful. We would sing songs, while I did her hair and she would be happy at least for a time.

I was now in junior high and I heard my Dad outside and I woke my Brother and Sister with a whisper, "Let's go into my room and sleep. Ok?" They were so little, but they knew enough to whisper back, "Ok". This night I waited until he got close to the door with her. He was slamming her head against the door and choking her. I could hear her gasping for breath. The door wouldn't open. I heard him slamming her head. I told my Brother and Sister to pretend they were asleep. They slipped under the covers. I got on my knees and began to pray. He opened the door and I could hear him choking my Mother. I could hear him breathing, heavy, monstrously. I continued to pray. He had moved her into their bedroom. I got up from my knees but raised prayer

Why whisper?

hands and began to pray for my Mother. She was screaming, "NO! NO! NO!" She was gagging and he was yelling, "How about that!!" I heard her clothing rip...she was whimpering now!"

I sat on the side of my bed waiting. I heard him jump in the shower. He was slamming doors and drawers. I smelled him put on his Old Spice cologne. He always wore too much! I hated Old Spice then and I hate it now. He slammed out of the house and sped away in the car.

I stood up and prayed. "God give me strength to take care of my Mother." I was tired and had to go to school in three hours. I opened her door and she was whimpering. "Mommy, I love you." I went into the bathroom and got a warm rag. I came back into the room which reeked of blood, skin and sex and I began to wipe her face. Her clothes were ripped up and her body was bruised. One of her eyes was swollen and black. She looked at me and said, "He keeps hurting me, but I love him. I don't know what I've done to deserve this. He just keeps hurting me." I kept cleaning her up until she was washed clean. I got her a gown to put on and put her in her bed. She was still crying, and I rubbed her hair and put the cover over her. I kissed her on her forehead until she fell asleep.

Charismatic Violence

The bathroom and the house were bloody. I had resigned myself to the fact that I was going to be without sleep. I looked in on my Brother and Sister. Then, I understood that like most nights, I had to clean.

UNCLE BROTHERS

I had often referred to my uncles as my Uncle Brothers. On both sides the Uncles were young, but most had a hand in raising or watching me. They were my examples, my rocks, my protectors. They were the ones who made me feel that God had placed in my life, men who would kill for me if need be, and maybe they had.

Uncle Evan

Uncle Evan had always been around when I was growing up. He was thin and handsome. He was always there to let me know that I was a beautiful girl and what love felt like from a man who sincerely cared about me being a success. He told me he loved me like his own Daughter since the day I was born. He would send me a picture of him, and I would always put it on my dresser. It reminded me that I could do anything because Uncle Evan said so.

He didn't talk a whole lot, but when he did it was important. He would answer my questions about boys, without yelling at me. I remember asking him about this boy at school who wanted to sleep with me. I was only in sixth grade. My Uncle Evan told me to tell him that if he really loved me he would wait until I graduated from High School. So that became my standard. "I would tell guys that they would have to wait for me until I graduated from high school." He would tell me the things that guys would say when they wanted to be with me or how to recognize the players or the guys that did not care about me.

I would sometimes call him out of the blue to ask about things that I knew he would know about. Sometimes I was surprised when I found out he knew a lot about what was going on in my life. He was to me...a genius. All of his advice was on the money. How did an Uncle know so much? When I was young I asked him once, "Uncle Evan, how do you know so much, you're a boy?"

Uncle Wade

He says, he used to babysit me. He says he was the one who would take me on the horseback rides when I was young. I do remember riding up and down a street named

Uncle Brothers

Prairie on a horse. It was fun and I remember feeling safe. My Uncle Wade was another one who would tell me about guys. I believe it started the first day he realized I was wearing a bra. I heard him asking my Mom, "Hey is this girl wearing a bra?" My Mom said…"Yes Wade, she is growing up." Uncle Wade replied, "Well it's too soon for my taste."

Then he began the Q and A with me. "Hey! So, what are the boys saying about you?" I looked at Uncle Wade like he was an older Brother and said…"Whaaaaat?" He pushed me…"Tell them boys I am going to kill them." I was like "No, Uncle Wade". He said "No…seriously…tell them, "Boy, if you try to kiss me, my Uncle Wade said he will kill you."…He was laughing. Uncle Wade was always messing with someone… kidding around, but I don't think he was kidding that day. I used to like when I would hang with Uncle Wade because he was cool, charismatic. He was always smart and said words people did not understand. I did though and he would look down at me and laugh. They didn't know what I was talking about, did they? I would giggle and say, 'No." Then he would say ,"Ok then, what did I mean?" And I would tell him." If I was right, he would smile and say, "Yep." but, if I was wrong he would say, "Look it up." Uncle Wade was the reason I kept reading. He said, "Reading will help you understand what people are talking about...always read and sometimes you can even figure out what the word means by reading the sentence. I wanted to be smart like him.

Uncle Josh

Uncle Josh was always giving me these silly nicknames, but it was cool; or he would add a nickname to a nickname. My nickname was Poopsie, but he would call me Poopsie Woopsie. That was cool until I became a teenager then I was like "Uncle Josh!" He used to like to walk into the teenage girl conversations.

Occasionally, there was a family get together and I would be hanging out with my cousin Darla, or Sandy or Tanya...just depended on who was over. Uncle Josh would walk up and say something like..."What's going on over here?" We would all roll our eyes or say something like "go away" of course playfully. He would always know "exactly" what we were talking about. "I know you girls are talking about boys! Boys, Boys, Boys! Ya'll are all boy crazy but...hmm...let's see...Probably some ole skinny boy who runs around in a tank top told one of ya'll you was fine or how he liked your skirt or the outfit you had on. One of ya'll just broke up with a boy and now you hate him and the other one is mad because one of the girls you hang out with at school stole your boyfriend. Well...here it is! The boy who is walking around looking like a skeleton in a tank top is only complimenting you because he is looking at your behind or your legs and he is just trying to get some. He can't possibly be serious about you because he doesn't even have a job! The one who just broke up with her boyfriend is the smart one...ya'll are too young to be thinkin about having boyfriends right now...wait until your last year in college and meet him in college and get you a boyfriend and then that way you will know he is about something. That last situation means he doesn't even care about himself. A guy that cheats on you obviously does not care about you, but that means he doesn't care about himself either. If he can't control himself against your friends, then he is probably not going to know how to take care of himself or his family." We all had eyes open as big as quarters. "My cousin Sandy waived him off, "Go away Cousin Josh!" He was Sandy's first cousin and she was my second. Uncle Josh laughed as he walked away. When he got far enough away not to hear us, we said at the same time, "But he was right!"

Uncle Clyde

To me, Uncle Clyde was always this tall man. I used to think he was tall because he was supposed to work with horses. As a little girl, I thought, God made him tall so he can talk to the horses to their faces. Uncle Clyde was always smiling and laughing at people that Grandma would yell at. He would tease them, and my Mother's brothers and sisters were always saying, "Shut up Clyde". Uncle Clyde was not around as much as my other uncles; but I do remember this. Uncle Clyde would stop whatever it was he was doing to sit down or bend down to talk to me about whatever my issue was.

He made me feel so important. I remember being about five or six and someone had yelled at me. I was sitting on the porch crying. He came and sat down next to me and said, "What's going on pretty girl?" He had no idea how he was pouring into my self-esteem. I looked up at him in tears and I am sure I told him some story of being victimized by an adult. I remember him saying, "Well they are just wrong because you are perfect in every way. You are the best niece I have ever had." I think I may have been the only niece at that time. "He asked me if I wanted to walk through the park and I nodded yes. He took the handkerchief out of his pocket and wiped my face.

As we were walking I looked up at him and told him I was sorry for messing up his napkin. He smiled and kept looking forward and he said, "You are my favorite girl. Let me tell you some things and you will understand when you get older. A good man will always hand you his napkin if you are crying. A man who respects you will take off his hat when he is talking to you and if it's rainy and cold and a man takes off his jacket and puts it on you then he is on track to be a good man. But if he does not do any of those things, you kick him to the curb." I was confused. "But Uncle Clyde, I'm too little to kick a man to the curb!" Uncle Clyde laughed so hard he sat down on the sidewalk. A week before my Uncle Clyde died I left him a voicemail telling him I loved him and that I wanted to talk to him. I told him I wanted for him to get better so we could talk soon. He called me back and left a message, "Hey Poopsie, I guess it's Yvonne now...you're grown, beautiful like your Momma. It was great to hear from you and I am working on that 'get better'! Call me back. Love you too!" I didn't get a chance to call him back because he died. I live with that in my heart every day.

Uncle Vyn

Uncle Vyn was smooth jazz. He seemed to understand us all the way and whenever Momma would hang out with her friends in California, Uncle Vyn would watch us. We had a tradition...potatoes! There were three of us, and of course Uncle Vyn, who was over six feet. Skinny but tall, Uncle Vyn would talk to us about life while he peeled potatoes and he would pretty much peel most of the ten-pound bag.

While he was peeling, he was telling us about life. How we should always stick together, how we should love family and how we shouldn't judge people. He would put all those potatoes in a pot and season it with only salt and pepper, but they were the best potatoes ever.

While the potatoes were cooking, Uncle Vyn would take us downstairs and have us sit down. He was still life coaching us when he pulled out his weed box and began rolling a joint. We learned the philosophy of Marijuana and the school of joint rollin'. He was very stern when he pointed out that we were not allowed to touch, nor participate in these festivities. Uncle Vyn would never get high in front of us but would send us upstairs to watch "The Monkees" while he took part in his own relaxation. When he came back upstairs it was time for more life coaching and he told us how to light incense to keep the smell from being all over the house. Grandma would sometimes come home and yell, "Vyn, have you been smoking that stuff in this house?!" He would always yell, "No Momma!" If I was with her she would look down and say, "I know he is smoking that stuff. I'm going to catch him one day." I would give her the blank look and would never tell on Uncle Vyn.

Uncle Vyn was our Cooley High, our Ride or Die. I remember we would ask him a series of questions that he always answered with, "Because I'm cool." "Uncle Vyn why is your ear pierced?" "Because I'm cool." "Uncle Vyn why are your shoes so long?" "Because I'm cool." "Uncle Vyn why do you wear your hat over your eye?" "Because I'm cool." "Uncle Vyn why do you have on pants with animals on them" "Because I'm cool."

There is a picture of me in front of my Grandma's house. I have a shirt on with birds on it and a pair of pants on with birds on them. My hat is tilted to the side...because like Uncle Vyn...I wanted to be cool.

ON KILLING YOUR COUSIN

My mom kept making me play with Einah, but for the most part I hated her. She would always beat me up, torture me in some way and take whatever self-esteem I had and try to destroy it. She reminded me consistently how "ugly and black" I was. She would tell me that I had no shape and no breasts when I was in junior high and that I was going to be a maid or something like that. It was then, I decided quietly that I would operate and own my own business. Of course, I would never tell her that.

Every so often she would throw food at me or put gum in my hair or some other thing that made her laugh out loud. One time she grabbed two of the clotheslines and put one on each side of my neck. I wasn't even aware she had done it until the clotheslines lifted me up in the air by my neck. I was choking. I was trying to pull the lines off my neck and Einah was standing there laughing. All of a sudden I fell to the ground.

On Killing Your Cousin

Einah's Mom had rescued me. I told this time and I told well, and I told about all of the things that Einah had done to me. Einah's Mom ordered her in the house. I went in also, but since I walked in first Einah tripped me and I fell and skinned my elbows and my hands. Einah laughed again and then she stopped, and her eyes were as big as quarters; and then I remembered why I never told on Einah, no matter what she did.

Einah's mom pulled out an old iron cord. She began to beat Einah in the back with the cord, but Einah would not cry. After a while, I could see blood on the shirt but Einah would not cry. Her Mom was calling her every name in the book but what happened next would live in my mind forever. Her mom reached in the cabinet in the kitchen and pulled out a cast iron pot from the cabinet. Einah's Mom hit her in the back with a full swing and Einah fell to her knees. She was now crying; she was hunched over holding her arms together. I began to cry and that stopped Einah's Mom from hitting her again. She left the kitchen, calling Einah every name in the book.

I helped Einah up and walked with her to the bathroom. I took a warm washcloth and washed her face and her back. She had stripes on her back from where the skin had been removed. For one moment, Einah looked into my eyes and whispered through tears, "Thank you".

We went into their family room and watched TV.

I never told on Einah again. Even when she pushed me in the pool, knowing I could not swim. There were other times Einah got in trouble, but most times it was with her Father. He would make her go into his bedroom and she would be in there for over three hours. She would always come out with tears streaming down her face. She would not talk for a long time but would always start cleaning the house and doing whatever chores, since her mom was at work. We were to find out later that Einah was being sexually abused by her Father.

ON SWINGING

There had been this talk, this gossip about swinging, about sexual deviation and abuse in the family; but no one would really admit it was happening. As Children we were left alone a lot and it seemed that the adults really thought they were hiding things from us, but we always found out.

As Cousins, we were sworn to secrecy, but whomever's home we were left at for the night had the opportunity to provide "show and tell" to the rest of the group.

One house provided a night of looking at naughty magazines. They included, Women only, Men only, Women with Women, Men with Men, group sex, animal and humans, that drawer was a regular Sodom and Gomorrah of magazines.

The second house provided the top drawer of goodies. Inserts, outputs, in all colors. Things that beeped and rotated. That drawer smelled terrible when you opened it, so the fascination with those items didn't last very long! As young kids we asked each other questions like, "Where does THAT go?" and "That seems awfully big to fit into anything!" Nevertheless, the discovery was to be a secret carried to the grave.

The third house contained pictures in the top drawer. Which received a big...Uhhhhhhhggh! There were all kinds of nude pictures of all kinds of things, parts of the body that we only associated with waste. We never looked at my Aunt and Uncle the same. We all giggled when they came home from going out.

The fourth house was where we hit the jackpot. Nothing in the drawers...hmmm...we knew there was something...somewhere! We hit the closet and one of the cousins waived us over..."Look guys. What's in here?"

The Shoe box had a bunch of black video cassettes with xx's on them. We knew how to play a video recorder, so we turned it on and put the first one in. We sat transfixed by the videos. We were so enthralled in them that we did not hear the car pull up. When the key hit the lock, someone yanked out the video and another one of us shoved the box under the couch. The other four of us sat on the floor in front of the video box so the parents could not see it. Cousin Beewee decided to take the hit for all of us and went into the kitchen and acted like he accidentally dropped and broke a glass. Of course, all the adults ran into the kitchen and while he acted like he was hurt, two of us ran and put the video box back where it was.

We smiled when we came back out and Bee Wee said he felt fine after all. Driving home, my Brothers and Sisters and I were giggling, thinking about what we had all gotten away with. What we did not know was that all the things we were being exposed to at seven and eight were only additional examples of child abuse.

We were at the store giggling about the videos again when I happened to look up at my Mother. It was just before dusk, and the evening sun was hitting her face. It was coming through the brown wig she had on and had created this beautiful color on her face.

She was walking past people and they were staring at her. She was super beautiful this day and although people were looking at her, she was looking at the floor. It was in the pasta aisle that I sat on the floor and looked up at her. "Yvonne, get off that nasty floor!"

Charismatic Violence

I stayed on the floor, "Mommy", I whispered, "Look up, Mommy. People are looking at you because you are so beautiful." It was like she had never heard that before. My Mom looked up and saw the man at the end of the aisle tip his hat to her. She nodded. She looked back at me with a question mark in her face. She walked slowly now and watched people watch her. Some people smiled and she would give them a half smile. When we were grabbing eggs, a gentleman walked up to my Mother and said, "Has your Husband told you that you are beautiful today?. My Mother whispered, "No." The man shook his head and walked away.

I was still looking up at my Mother when she bent down in front of me in the aisle. She took my face in her hands and said, "I love you. You are one of the best mistakes I ever made."

LEAVE MY HUSBAND ALONE

I remember it being late when the doorbell rang. It was a cool doorbell for an apartment. The type of doorbell that sang its own song when it rang. My Nanna was staying the weekend with us because my Dad had been told by the police to leave the house ...again. It was my Aunt Sara at the door. She was in a purple leather outfit and she actually looked nice. She had a wig on that smelled like alcohol and cigarette smoke. I think they just didn't see me. I was standing behind my Mother's right leg when Aunt Sara pulled out the gun. Aunt Sara was pointing it at my Mother's face. "Stay away from my Husband." My Mother didn't flinch. She just stood there staring at my Aunt Sara. I think she was tired of living anyway. I think that in her mind she wanted my Aunt Sara to kill her...to take her out of her misery.

My Nanna pulled my Mother back and stood in front of her. Nanna was only five foot four, but her presence was big. She whispered to my Aunt Sara, "Sara...don't do this...you have children and so does Fleta. This is not true, and I don't know where you are getting this craziness from?" Aunt Sara lowered the gun, "Her husband told me that he suspected she was sleeping with MY husband. He told me I should kill her for it. Of course, then he asked me if he could sleep with ME."

My Nanna took a deep breath and grabbed my Aunt Sara's free hand. "Come here baby and let's talk about this crazy man and his psychosis." She led my Aunt Sara to the couch and sat her down next to my Mom. With the same gentle movement, she took the gun from my Aunt Sara. My Mother was sitting on the couch and I was holding her hand, standing on the side of the couch.

My Mother was staring at the front door and her voice took on the low sinister sound I had only heard once before, "If you ever bring a gun to my house where my children are I will place my fingers around your throat and squeeze until I crush every bone. Are we clear?" Her head turned to my Aunt Sara like the Lisa Blair in the exorcist. I could tell my Aunt Sara was scared. She looked at my Mom with pop bottle eyes now. She was not the Woman who had pulled the gun at the door just ten minutes ago.

Leave My Husband Alone

My Mother looked at my Aunt Sara and growled, "Get the hell out of my house." My Aunt Sara was crying. My Mother gave her no mercy. "Whatever it is that you are suffering with Dego, then you deserve it! You stole him from me and so now you need to get the hell out of my house." Dego was my Father's friend and actually was my Mother's boyfriend first. My Aunt Sara was walking toward the door and my Nanna was consoling her. She kept telling her to pray and give it to God. Nanna told Aunt Sara to call her when she got home and then she closed the door.

After Aunt Sara left, Nanna turned to Momma and said, "What were you talking about? Dego? What did you mean?" My Mother sighed like she was irritated and then she began to tell the Story.

"I was the first to date Dego. He was perfect for me. We had intelligent conversations and he was sooo fine to me." (Uncle Dego had green eyes and was a very classy man…in a pimp sort of way) We would talk every day and he would tell me that I was beautiful and that he would always love me. We were already talking about getting married. One day Sara was over my house and Momma told me to go wash the dishes. I told Sara to talk to him while I went in to do the dishes real quick. When I came back, Sara told me he said he had to go.

I found out later that Sara had told him that I said I did not want to ever talk to him ever again...and then she gave him her number, so he started calling her. Well, she was dating him secretly and then got pregnant by him. I did not even know his last name; so, when she told me she was getting married I did not know it was him. After I got married I went to Charles' Mom's house and realized he was Charles' friend and I freaked out. He told me what Sara did and we both cried. We have not touched each other since, but he should have been MY husband and the Father of MY children." My Nanna took her hand and told her she had to forgive. My Mother just sat there looking into space. "If I wanted him I could have him, but I will not do to other women what women have done to me."

It was then they realized that I had been standing there the whole time. "Girl what are you doing up? Get to bed." My Nanna was kind of giggling and she grabbed my hand to take me to my room. I leaned over to kiss my Mother goodnight. "Good night Mommy." She turned to me with a warm smile..."Mommy loves you and I will NEVER, EVER let anybody hurt you and if they do...I will make sure they suffer the consequences!" And she did. My Mother always shared with me to protect my own Children the way she did, and I did...always. We never did find that gun.

OTHER

I was talking to a dear friend from one of my church groups and she relayed to me that whenever a child experiences devastating pain, it is at that age they hold inside them that pain to adulthood. It was then that I realized that I was consciously four years old. Making up for people, making excuses for pleasing others...even at the detriment of myself. I determined that today at 48 years old I was going to tell the truth. I was going to be honest and transparent. I was going to tell exactly how I felt about things. Not to be hurtful, but to be free from always accommodating and always pleasing. It was not until I was in the church group that I realized that I had that disease, pleasing people. It was as if God was now finally teaching me, training me to be the person he wanted me to be; and the lessons were hard, hurtful because they meant "I" had to change. Pastor Gaylon Clark at Greater Mount Zion Church in Austin, Texas had begun to preach my healing from the

Other

first Sunday I was there. His inspiration and honestly led me to the tears I needed to cry in order to forgive.

In the meantime, God was speaking not only through church but also through Oprah and Iyanla. They were helping me through their life classes to understand that the choices I was making, the way I was living my life was "my choice". I was still living this because "I had chosen to do so". I had to change it.

I realized when I was talking to the counselor about being young, that I was always trying to give my Mom something to be proud of. My Mother was constantly shamed by my Father's family. They often blamed her for the abuse she suffered. Her side of the family looked at her "with" shame because they couldn't understand why she would stay in "that" situation. It is an agreement with my life to have what 'I" want, what "I" enjoy, and what "GOD" kept telling me all those years I could have, wondering…how did I get here? what am I learning and what will I take with me in the future?

I am smiling, "I" loved her, and I did not care if anyone else did! I was going to do it for the rest of my life…make sure that she was always able to brag.

Be an example for my little Sisters. Early on, we knew that the trauma had caused both of them great pain. Praying they would seek counseling but loving them both to the next level and the next and the next. Praying they would understand their Big Sister, once and for all, and tell their own stories, not mine, honestly.

A BITING AUNTIE

I never knew what she was going to do when I saw her, but I knew she wouldn't let me down. She was consistent in making sure that she did something mean, and it always left an impression. She had enough intelligence to destroy the self-esteem of one of us...my Mother or me, whenever she could.

Today she walked in and actually hugged my Mom. I saw my Mom sigh as if grateful not to be the victim...or at least for now. My Aunt Norina was about 5'9, dark, with short hair. She was mannish in the face and smiled way to hard. She was always talking about the fact that her hair wouldn't grow, and I figured it was because she was so snide.

After hugging everyone in the living room, she looked across the room at me. "Oh, I see your Mom dressed you decent for once. You always did look like a little boy anyway! Come here and give your aunt Norina a kiss. I stood up, not smiling and walked slowly over to her. She smiled at me with an eery smile and then, when I thought she was only going to kiss my cheek, she bit it. She took a big piece of my cheek into her mouth and bit down as hard as she could. She took a little piece of my skin with it. It hurt so much my eyes began to water.

She began to laugh an evil laugh and I stood there sniffling as water ran down my face from both eyes. "Oh, you are going to be ok, little black ugly thang. I can't believe she was crying!! She better be glad I showed her any affection at all." She was a demon and I was trying to figure out how she operated every day with such evil residing in her. She liked the movie "The Exorcist" and I was not surprised.

THE CONCERT

My Aunt Norina was mean and would often bring her friends to hook up with my Father when he was playing in the band. When my Father got back home to Colorado from California he had it in his mind to get back to singing in his old band. The band came back together and before we knew it things were back to crazy.

It was the first time I had ever watched my Dad sing in public. He was really good. We had a table at the dance floor and because we were his children we were able to watch our Dad sing. We danced and had fun. Mom was wearing a wig to cover up her bruises and sitting at the table patiently as women went up to my Dad on stage and planted kisses on him. Some of them even looked back at her as if to torture her.

Most of the women were from town so they knew he beat her, but they didn't care and like just about everyone else they deemed the beatings her fault. Of course, my Aunt Norina led the charge.

That night my Father got off the stage and came over and grabbed my Mom's hand. He took her to the floor and danced one fast song and one slow song with her. He never told the crowd that she was his wife, nor did he give her any additional acknowledgement.

I was waiting for him to do so, but he never did. He did, however, acknowledge me. He was singing a slow song and asked, "Who wants to dance with me?" The women were screaming. He pushed through them and on the way handed his fellow singer, Floyd, the mike. He came over to me and placed me on his feet. I was about nine years old. He danced and I followed, standing on his feet for every move. People were taking pictures and women were falling more in love with him. My Mom was crying...she was proud of that moment. We were able to stay until my Dad came over and said, "It's eleven, you and the kids need to go up to the room and go to bed." My Mom asked, "Well when are you coming up?" He immediately became angry. Gritting his teeth, he said, "Get upstairs now!" Mom grabbed us and headed upstairs.

The Concert

He came to the room later with two white women. He instructed them to sit on the bed and he told my Mom to get in the bathroom. The white Women were trying to occupy us, telling us how cute we were.

They sat there, trying to laugh with us…telling us how cute we were as they heard my Mom scream for her life. He beat her for a good twenty minutes and when he was done he came out of the bathroom, shirt ripped and covered with blood.

They looked at each other. He said, "Let me just change my shirt and we can go." They both began to giggle. He took off his shirt and put on another one.

"Yvonne help your Mom!" He yelled back over his shoulders as he held both of the women around their waists. I could hear them giggling with my Dad as they walked down the hall.

I put his shirt in the trash can. I was hoping someone would see the blood on the shirt and maybe try to investigate what had happened.

I told my Brother and Sister to take off their outfits and get in the bed. I told them to cover their faces with the covers and go to sleep, or else Dad would get mad. They both got undressed, said their prayers and lay on the sofa bed with the covers over their faces. I simply did not want them to see my Mom... however, she looked.

I walked slowly around the corner. One of my Mom's legs was hanging out of the bathtub. It was covered in blood. I walked up to the tub sliding from the blood on the floor. She was moaning. I immediately turned on the sink. I grabbed a white washcloth and pulled the shower curtain from her face. The right side of my Mother's face was disfigured. Elephantitis big. The first time I had seen her face like this I had winced...it had scared me. Now I was used to the image and as long as she was not dead I knew I could be strong.

I continued to wipe her face and hair; she wasn't flinching. She was so swollen she could not even feel me cleaning her up. Somehow I lifted her up and she knew to walk to the bed. I had already placed towels on the bed so I could wash her body. I removed her clothes. She was so thin...her body covered in black and blue bruises, scratches...blood. I could smell him on her, his body, his sweat and sex. He had raped her before he left. I was used to that too.

The Concert

After I washed her off and dried her body. I put on her pajamas. She rolled to her side and curled up in a fetal position. I kissed her on her forehead. "I love you Mommy."

"She muttered, "I love you too."

FIGHTING MY DAD
ABOUT COLLEGE

I was watching Obama's reelection speech when I thought about my battle to go to college. I was thinking about the American people and how we had done what was right. We had voted for the people who were working hard, the people who needed a break, a leg up. We had voted for all races, for all creeds and all colors, we had voted for women, we had voted for men, we had voted for our military. We had voted to help each other, to stay in America at least for four more years, that wanted to see each other successful. I was grateful to Obama for the ability to pay for my daughter's insurance, for the idea that perhaps I could get a break paying for my daughter's college tuition. I was grateful for the next four years and I remembered my conversation with my Father about going to College.

I had come home after school, excited about getting letters from colleges all over the nation. My counselor had

Fighting My Dad about College

told me two things that morning. She said, "I am so proud of you. Because you have done so well...you are representing our school as an Owl Club Debutante and I have some acceptance letters for you." I said but I only applied to two schools. She said, "I know but I paid some of the application fees." I could not believe it. She gave me a letter from Brown, a letter from Howard, one from University of Denver and then recruiting pamphlets with my name on them from Harvard, Yale... and the list goes on.

I had always wanted to go to Howard. It was my dream and so now I had to go home and ask my parents to help me get there. I figured if they would just help me get the bus money or plane fare to get there...well I could do the rest. I knew God would help me...if I could just get there.

I cried all the way home on the city bus. All my hard work had paid off. All the organizations I was involved in that I had dedicated my life towards were finally paying off. I knew my parents were going to be proud. I knew this was going to be an awesome night.

When I walked in I felt the tension. My father had on his white tank top and my Mom was already crying. He was belittling her as usual. "Because you're a stupid b......" She was leaned up against the wall and he was in her ear yelling".

Somehow I thought my good news would change the tide of the evening. I thought if I yelled out the good news...he would stop the madness and focus on me. "Dad!" I yelled. I am going to college!"

He turned to me slowly. I smiled at him, "Dad, I am going to college! My counselor helped me! She applied at some colleges and I didn't even know it!" He was moving slowly towards me...I kept smiling at him...I was thinking it was working...he was moving away from my Mom...it was working. I continued..." Dad and I am also a debutante Dad...look at this letter! Isn't that cool?" He took the letter out of my hand and began to read it. I continued excitedly, "Look Dad...the AKA's gave me a scholarship...some money towards school...Look!" He took the letter and read it and said..."ummm hmmmm". I asked him..."Well Dad what do you think?"

He handed me back the letter and looked me right in the eyes. "I think you are going to be a whore like your Mom! I think you are going to be pregnant because you have opened your legs and you are going to have some baby that you didn't plan to have! Your Mom was a whore! We didn't plan you! But I did the right thing and married her anyway! My Dad forced me because she was pregnant he said, "Boy, you

Fighting My Dad about College

are gonna do right by that girl since you got her pregnant! That's how we got you...we didn't plan you...we didn't want you! But since you were up inside your Mom we just did the right thing!"

I had pulled some strength from somewhere and I whispered, "I am a virgin." He yelled in my face, "WHatcha say?!" I said, "I am a virgin." He was on me now. His breath was on my face...occasionally I felt the spit from his mouth. I didn't dare move, although I wanted to wipe it off. "Oh, so you think that makes you better than everybody else? Miss Honor Roll, miss Drill Team captain. Don't nobody give a shit about that. Miss too good to get high with the rest of the family. Too good to have a drink. I asked you to have a damn beer with me and you said, "No daddy I have to study!" Well, take your ass on then Miss High Sadity...I don't give a fuck! You are going to stop going to those meetings and activities too. Quit that damn job too! From now on you are in this house all day before school and after school!"

I whispered, "Dad if I stop my activities I won't get my scholarship to college." He laughed, "Well Ms. High Sadity, what you gonna do now?" At that point I felt defeated and had nothing to lose. I wanted him to feel the pain I had felt. I wanted him to see how it felt when someone spoke to you with malice and loathing. It came from somewhere deep in my soul. It came from years of being silent. It came from years of cleaning up blood and mess and listening to him yell and scream and break things.

I opened my mouth and said, "WELL YOU CERTAINLY CANNOT AFFORD TO SEND ME TO COLLEGE, BECAUSE THE ONLY PLANS YOU HAVE EVER MADE WERE ABOUT HOW YOU WERE GOING TO DO DRUGS OR CHEAT AND BEAT ON MOM!!!"

Before I knew what hit me....he already had. I remember the punch to my face and how the pain was so much that I went numb. I had been hit so hard my feet had left the ground and I had hit the living room wall. It was the first time he had hit me since I was a child. He wanted to make a point with this hit.

I felt the pain and it was so much that I couldn't even scream. My lungs were stuck in slow motion and it felt like the scream came from deep in my soul. At that moment, I felt my Mother's pain. The anguish that she would feel every time he hit her. How had she done it all these years?

I got myself up and went to the bathroom. He was screaming at the bathroom door. Calling me every name in

Fighting My Dad about College

the book...whore, slut and anything else he could think of. He was reminding me how I was not going to be anything....how I was not going to be anything except a pregnant whore...I was crying in the bathroom...watching my face in the mirror turn from red to blue to black. I was watching my lip and cheek grow and my eye close. I was in excruciating pain. How did my Mom do it? How did she tolerate him beating on her every day?

I heard him eating...slamming the fork on the plate...criticizing my Mother's cooking. I came out of the bathroom and he called me over..." Hey...get over here!" I could barely walk. I came around the corner. He looked at me like he was in shock. He sat there with his mouth open...it was as if he didn't know what had just happened.

He began to cry. He threw his food tray and plate on the floor. He grabbed his keys off the wall and left the house. My mom was crying, picking up the food and tray off the floor. She looked up at me for a moment and said she was sorry. She was sobbing.

I left the living room and headed to my room. In my room I sat on my bed and began to figure out what my strategy would be for school. I didn't want to call in sick, so I thought it would be a good idea to wear sunglasses.

I asked my mom if she had some sunglasses I could wear. She said yes and we both figured things would be ok. The glasses and a little make-up would cover it. We both agreed that I was a good student, so no one would pay attention to me anyway. We just knew it. That is not what happened!

Immediately upon entering my first class, my teacher asked..."Yvonne what is wrong?" I answered matter of factly..."Oh nothing...I was up late last night, and my eyes are real sensitive today." She looked at me. She left the class and came back about 10 minutes later.

FORT MORGAN

My counselor was a short round woman with pale skin. You could tell she was a "small town wife" who had taken the job at South to get some "culture" on her resume. She was our "Ms. Daisy" with her own preconceptions about how Black people really were but she could certainly rescue any Black children because she was better, more powerful, white. She was pale, pasty and did not "know" any of her students. Coming into her office, she would never listen to your concerns and she really didn't remember who or what student she had spoken to, or about what. By my senior year, I knew how to manage her.

When I first started at South in my Sophomore year, Patsey told me she had already planned out my next three years. She told me she would focus me on Future Homemakers classes and things that would help me in my future career; only she hadn't asked me what my career aspirations were. I simply nodded. I looked at the classes and asked her when she would be available to actually talk and she said she would be out for the next couple of days. Perfect! The next morning, I came into the office and told them Ms. Pastey had said some of my classes were supposed to be changed, but I did not see the changes on my classes. The school office clerk said, "Oh my," and went about the business of asking me what classes I was supposed to have. I told her I was supposed to have all AP classes and she changed them all except for the FHA class. I still needed to know how to cook and how to sew.

When I met with Ms. Pastey the following year she seemed confused about the classes I had taken the previous year. "I think we made a grave mistake! You did well, but we have to adjust you back down to the classes you are supposed to be taking." "Ok." I didn't argue with her. I just waited until she was out of town and changed my schedule again.

My Junior year I was part of honor society and a "Who's Who amongst students" and Ms. Pastey seemed totally confused. "How is this happening!!?? I had it all planned out for you." I didn't know what she had planned, and I didn't ask. I left the office and of course returned not only to change my schedule, but to get a signature from a different counselor which allowed me to leave school for events, since I had now become a state officer for FHA.

Today, however I was in her office. My teacher had decided to ask me to pull off my sunglasses in class and I had told her no. She asked me to step out into the hall and when she did that is when I took off my glasses. She gasped to see my right eye closed, blue and black. I could not open it. She asked me what happened, and I could have lied, maybe I should have lied. I could have said I got in a fight or I could have said I had a crazy boyfriend, but I didn't. I told her the truth, thinking she would let me go back into class, that she would understand what I had worked so hard for. That I had worked hard to get out of the prison known as my house!

Ms. Pastey walked in her office, shaking her head. "You know, I knew this was going to happen. I kept my hopes up that something positive would come out of this but now you are going to be faced with doing a maid service or something like what I thought in the first place. In my day, most were maids because things like this happen in these types of families." I didn't respond, like always. "I have already contacted social services and they are sending someone over to pick you up. So, you will need to go get your personal belongings out of your locker. They are going to be removing you from your home." I was thinking "Hallelujah! Maybe now I could sleep in peace and get even better grades than I was getting. This was going to be sweet release! Maybe a foster home or something. I was old enough to take care of myself, just needed a place to crash.

When the social worker came I actually hugged her, thinking that she was going to take care of me, but she began to explain that I would be leaving South and would be enrolled in a temporary school, until the end of the year. Since I only had a month left of my junior year it would not be a bad thing. I was nodding.

Ms. Pastey gave her my file, "She was a great student, honors classes and community involvement and all, but these families are generally not successful after a while which is why I am recommending the child group home."

Child Group Home!! What is she talking about!? I began to cry. Ms. Pastey touched my shoulder, "Coming from the south I know you should not have got your hopes up, girl, thinking you could change the order of things. That's why"...I interrupted her as I walked out the door with my counselor. I pointed at her, "First, don't ever touch me again and don't tell me what I can or cannot do. Second, you are wrong." I walked out of her office and down the front steps of the school. When I got to the curb the counselor said, "I will go get my car and pull up." I looked back at South and said, "I'm not done with you yet."

We pulled up to the gate and I was relieved at first because I felt that my Dad would not be able to come for me because of all the security. I was looking for the good in it. When we pulled up to the group home, the front desk coordinator walked over to me with attitude face.

She explained to me that the kids here had been "problems in school, been arrested, had been deviants and one had tried to kill his parents in their sleep." The counselor interrupted, "She is not here for any of those reasons, Yvonne is here for protection." "Oh", the coordinator sighed. The Social Worker motioned for me to take off my glasses. The coordinator gasped, " We don't have any way to accommodate that. But if she can pass her GED we can go to a judge and see if she can make herself emancipated." "Ok" the Social worker stood up. I have to go. Let me know if you need something." The counselor motioned for me to follow her.

I followed her up concrete steps and my room was at the end of the hall. I noticed the stairs right across from my door. I was hopeful that I could leave when I wanted knowing the steps were there. When we walked in the room I noticed how cold it was. One window with bars on it on the inside and the outside. Two sets of bars? Really?! The bed was more of a cot with a gray cover, stained but clean. The bed was pushed next to the window and there was a closet. No dresser drawers. The room was gray, the floor was gray the closet was gray with plastic hangers. They were gray. Who designed this room? It was depressing!!

The counselor turned to me. "Ok you will stay here today and tomorrow you will get up for breakfast. At breakfast, I will give you your assignment. Everyone here helps out so you will get chores just like the rest of us. Fill out these papers so we know where you are in relation to school. This will tell me what classes you have already taken and what we need to do to get you your GED." GED?! What the hell is she talking about?! My mind was going crazy. I'm going to Howard University; I don't care what nobody says! The counselor handed me the paperwork. "Ok."

The counselor walked out of the room and closed the door. The back of the door was white. Was this done to match the sheets? This was an insane asylum. I laughed at myself. That's when I heard the locks. One, two, three, four, five. Ok, I guess. Didn't know I was that much of a threat.

Fort Morgan

I laid down on the bed and watched the leaves of the tree blow outside my window. The rustling put me to sleep.

I woke up to the moon. Beautiful, shining down on me; like God himself let me know that He knew I was there in that crazy gray room. It was strange, but I felt protected locked in and away from the crazy stuff at home; and although I was worried about my Brothers and Sisters I was relieved to get a night where I could just sleep.

I woke up to the smell of bacon. It made me smile, reminded me of my Great Grandmother Johnnie. I was ready to deal with this day. I got on my knees and prayed. "God, you already know what it is. Help me to deal with whatever comes in the way you would have me deal with it."

An hour later, a male counselor entered my room and told me it was time to come down and meet my fellow housemates. You will help in the kitchen each day, so essentially you will help clean up the kitchen after breakfast, lunch and dinner. Me to my mind, "Welcome home Kizzy".

The kitchen was huge and there were at least 15 kids moving about. The counselor who looked like Evan Boy from the Waltons with glasses, told everyone to sit down. "This is our new housemate, Yvonne; she is going to be here until...

whenever. Treat her with respect and she will be helping out in the kitchen. Make sure you get to know her and... whatever." He walked out of the room. The whole room had stopped moving and all the kids were looking at me. A skinny blonde girl walked up to me, "Come on, let's go chill in the living room." I followed her; the room started moving again as the kids finished doing what they were doing before. As I walked by a Hispanic male threw a Lego at me. "Your next." I gave him a look of aggravation. I already knew he was stupid just by the way his hair was in his eyes. He was a Breakfast Club wanna be. I should have said, " You are NOT Judd Nelson!" But I didn't. I laughed to myself.

Skinny girl began to tell me how things worked around the house and told me that if I wanted weed or cigarettes she could see that I got some. She wanted to know who would be sending money to me while I was there. "Nobody knows I'm here." She frowned. I stood up, "I'm going to my room. I'm tired". "No can do. We are forced to stay down here until at least noon. It is their attempt to make us socialize. So, it's going to be games, boring conversations or TV. Pick your poison."

I sighed and sat down, "Are you serious?" "Yep, after lunch we have school from 1-4 and then you can go back in your room." "Ok." One of the kids yelled, "Everyone on kitchen duty needs to get in here. We are starting clean up." I was glad for clean-up. It gave me something to do. I volunteered to put away the dishes. The kids were all talking about outside time which apparently was once per week and how they could not wait until Thursday.

The lunch crew was coming in for food prep, so we were told to get out of the kitchen. After lunch, clean up was hurried and all the high schoolers were crowded into a bedroom which was filled with classroom desks. There was a blackboard on one wall where Evan Walton was writing the assignment questions. He gave me a book and pointed to the writing on the chalkboard. "Complete pages 134 to 144". He bent down and whispered, "Did you complete the paper you were given yesterday?" I handed him the paper out of my pocket. "You were in advanced classes. I probably will bore you with the remedial stuff I'm teaching. I don't understand why smart kids do dumb shit and end up in here." I didn't respond. He didn't know my story. I completed pages 134 to 164. I handed him the book a half an hour into class time, "I'm going to my room." He nodded.

I walked up the cement stairs to my room. I closed the door and locked myself in with my one lock. I lay on my bed and watched and listened to the tree leaves until I fell asleep. A knock on my door woke me up for dinner. When I opened my door, fake Judd was standing there. "Dinnertime." He followed close behind me down the stairs. He whispered, "When a man knows what he wants he takes it. You are what I want. You are going to give it to me, or I am going to take it. Your choice!" His giggle sent chills up my spine. All through dinner he kept smiling. His teeth were gross, and he had a cut on his forehead. I was genuinely scared.

After dinner we were returned to our rooms and locked in. One, two, three, four, five. I was locked in and felt safe. I drifted off to sleep. In the middle of the night I heard the stair door close. There was a quiet knock on my door. I walked over to the door. "Who is it?" That giggle sent chills up my spine. "It's me, chickadee." Fake Judd was at the door. I backed away. "Ahhhh the counselor is an alcoholic; he drinks himself to sleep...sleep little sheep." The door locks began to click. One, two, three...four. The turning stopped. He walked away from the door, giggling.

I shivered and picked up the bed and moved it in front of the door. If he tried to get in the bed would make a lot of noise and someone was bound to hear. I placed the mattress on the floor by the window and watched the tree leaves. God what are you doing? I thought I was going to be able to at least sleep here. I got on my knees and put my hands together on the ledge. God, I need to get out of here. I don't know what is going on, but I don't belong here. What are you trying to teach me? I believe in your promises Lord and I am asking you in the name of Jesus to get me out of here.

I woke up in the morning to the screeching sound of the bed scraping across the floor. "What the hell are you doing?" Evan boy was waking me up for breakfast. "Well I was…" I was about to tell Evan boy what happened when I saw "Fake Judd" standing behind him choking a doll. The doll had a pair of scissors lodged in its chest. "Put the bed back where it's supposed to be and get downstairs for breakfast." Evan Boy turned around to head downstairs. Fake Judd was gone, but the image I had just seen was fresh in my mind.

I shared it with skinny blonde, but she was aloof. "Yeah he has come in just about all the girls' rooms; but we just let him do whatever and leave. He tried to totally kill both his parents and set them on fire so it's like you can end up dead or just let him do what he wants. For the most part, it is ok I guess. It's just when he bites you that makes it hard." My eyes were watering.

During school, Fake Judd sat behind me and continued to let out that eery giggle. I would get a chill down my back each time. When it was time to leave the classroom Fake Judd whispered, "See you later, alligator."

Heading up to my room, I heard the doorbell ring. "Hi, we are here to pick up the new girl we brought in on Monday." "Ohhh, ok"...I heard him walking up the stairs. He peeked into my room, "Hey, some people are here to pick you up." I followed him down the stairs. When I got to the bottom, I saw my Aunt Katelyn, my Mother's Sister. "Hi baby, I came to get you." I ran to her and started crying. She was crying too. "It's gonna be alright. It's gonna be ok." She was hugging me back, patting me on my back. "Do you have anything you need to go get, any clothes?" "No maam". I was holding her hand like a little girl. As we walked toward the exit, Fake Judd placed himself at the door. I leaned over to him and whispered, "Get thee behind me Satan, damn demon!"

When we got in the car Aunt Katelyn shared with me how she had been looking for me for three days. She had received a call from my Mother and my Mother had told her that she was not "allowed" by my Father to bring me home. She told my Aunt Katelyn that she had no idea where I was,

Fort Morgan

but maybe it was better than living in the house with them. My Aunt Katelyn was not ok with that and had set out to do something about it. She said that in the three days she had found out where I was, had my Mom sign papers relinquishing custody of me and had gone to court to basically list herself as my custodial parent. I was forever grateful to my Aunt Katelyn and will remain forever grateful.

My Mother had broken my heart.

DEAL WITH THE DEVIL

Deal with the Devil – During the time we were in Oakland without my Father. My Mother had connected herself to a handsome man. He was blonde, tall, beautiful and blue eyed. A tall version of Robert Redford. My dad was in Colorado and pretty much M.I.A. again. He had packed up his things for the umpteenth time and left my Mom with nothing. He always took all the money right before everything was due when he left, so he had done it again. He had made sure that she did not have rent, public service bill money and had thrown the little bit of groceries we had out onto the lawn and of course the dogs were eating that. It was then My Mother decided that we should move to California with my Grandma and Grandpa. So, my Mother called up my Grandma and arrangements were made for us to catch the Greyhound bus to Richmond.

It was not long after working that my Mother met this Robert Redford look-alike and he began to pick her up from my Grandma's house. Grandma didn't mind him, but Grandpa always gave him 21 questions each time he showed up at the door. He didn't seem to be bothered by the questions and utilized his manners well while in front all of us.

He would often bring dinner for all of us and would give my Grandmother and my Mother money to make sure we had something to eat. When school was about to start in the winter he took us shopping for clothing and said, "Hey guys, make sure you get enough outfits for at least five days. So, he bought us five pair of shoes each, five outfits and five packages of underwear and socks. We were in heaven!

He was consistently gentle with us. When he talked to my Mother he always began the conversations with how beautiful her kids were. We all would stare at him, but rarely did we smile, even when he was buying something for us.

Mother did not go over to his house for at least three months after dating him. She said she wanted to date him in public first before she spent any private time with Him. We agreed.

One night he came over to my Grandmother's house and invited all of us over to his house for dinner. He said he was going to cook for all of us. My Grandfather said no, of course; and looked at my Grandmother in such a way that she knew she was not going either.

My Grandfather pulled my Mother to the side, "Baby, I do not think you should go over there or take the kids over there. You do not know him that well." My Mother breathed out, "He would never hurt me or the kids. He is way to kind for that." My Grandfather looked down at me, as my Mother walked past him. He handed me a piece of paper and I could feel coins inside. I put the package in my coat pocket.

When we walked outside we all sang at the same time, "Whoaaa!" He had a convertible Eldorado. The top was down, and we couldn't wait to ride.

We jumped in the back and all enjoyed the wind blowing on us, as we drove watching the sunset. The drive was a while and the ocean was dancing on the right side of us. It was a beautiful scene and we drove up the hills to his home. There was a gate and I remember wishing I could have a home with a gate and an amazing brick driveway. His home was amazing. There were 4 archways a huge front porch and a view that was breathtaking.

Deal With the Devil

He took us around the back to go in, so he could show us the pool. It was the first time we smiled, "Yayyy!" He was happy we were happy and smiled gently, "You guys are welcome to swim here anytime." We smiled at each other and immediately began to discuss when we wanted to come back and how we wished we had brought our swimsuits with us. The inside of the home was immaculate, contemporary and filled with pictures of African sunsets and African people. I thought, hmmm that makes sense. He just likes black people.

He cooked a wonderful dinner and although we thought he was rich, he confirmed that he had been given the money to start his life by his Father. Only $700,000 but he had to work a job for at least 3 years after college and, of course, graduate from college. He had chosen to work for a company that processed honey and once he received his money from his Father he had decided to make perfumes made with honey. He had been very successful in doing so.

He went on to say that he knew he loved our Mother and would do the same for us if she decided to marry him. We were all nodding our heads and Mom was giggling.

After dinner, he said he wanted us to head downstairs with him so we could hang out and watch TV. Of course, we were down for that.

He opened the basement door and we immediately noticed the wall color was black. Huh? As we descended the stairs, something did not feel right, and my Mother placed herself in front of us very quickly. She was the first to round the corner into his downstairs family room. She looked back at us with fear on her face. When we rounded the corner we first saw on one wall a poster of Satan and some sort of prayer poster on the wall directly next to the picture. I started praying that God would get us out of this!!

There were pictures of tortured women and children on the other walls. He put on some demonic sounding music and my Brother yelled, "Hey, I thought we were going to watch some movies!?" My Brother was so brave to be so young. The music was turned off. He put on some Stephen Spielberg movie and we were all huddled together on the couch.

I pulled out my piece of paper from Grandpa. It read, "Grandpa's phone number is 510-375-4657. Call me if anything weird happens and here is a quarter for a payphone."

Deal With the Devil

He told us to relax and that he was going to use the bathroom.

As soon as he closed the door my Mother whispered in my ear. Go upstairs and call your Grandma and Grandpa's house. Tell them you need them to call back this number and create an emergency so that we can go back home. Also look next to the phone and I noticed his address, tell your Grandma and Grandpa where we are.

I ran upstairs and made the call. I told Grandpa everything she said, and he said he would call back in five minutes. Before I hung up I said, "Oh and Grandpa, he has pictures of the devil and people being killed on his walls!!"

I went into the upstairs bathroom and flushed the toilet. When I came downstairs He was sitting there in an all-black robe. He had placed a bunch of sharp knives on a table behind the sofa we were sitting on. They were shiny, placed on a black handkerchief. My Brother and Sister looked terrified. My Mother looked calm and collected but I knew why, and I knew I had to act the same.

"Did you find the bathroom?" He looked up at me. "I did." I smiled at him and asked if he had the movie Ben with Michael Jackson. He nodded, "ok."

A few minutes later his phone rang. "Oh...oh no! Sure Mr. Wilson, I can make sure and bring them home right away. We will be there shortly. Oh...sure officer I completely understand. Yes sir. These things can certainly come without notice."

He hung up the phone. "Hey guys it seems someone has had an accident in your family, and I have to take you guys home. I guess the police officer at your Grandfather's house is there and wants to wait to tell you all the details when you are all together. Gather your things and I'll change and get your guys home. My Mother breathed out, "Hey, we are going to meet you outside at the car okay?" "Sure," see you guys at the car."

We all ran up the stairs, including Mom! We were all praying little prayers and telling each other to silently pray until we were safely back at Grandma and Grandpa's.

We were super quiet as we rode back home, and the ocean sounds were now crashing against our ears. It was cold and we wondered why he had not closed the convertible top.

He seemed to be calmly angered. He was being passive aggressive and asking my Mom how my Grandfather could have possibly known his phone number. My Mother responded," My Father is friends with many police officers, so I am not surprised he was able to find your information." He looked over at my Mother, "hmmm".

When we pulled up to the house two Richmond police officers were standing outside. They opened the door of the car, "Hey kids, you guys cold?" "Yessss!" All three of us hugged the officers before we ran into the house. I looked back for my Mother.

"Hey, I will call you later", She waved to him as he drove away quickly. When he rounded the corner, she collapsed to the ground crying. One of the officers bent down to help her, "Maam are you ok?" My Mother looked up at them, "Thank you so much!!" She was crying. "Hey, don't thank us, thank that man right there." Grandpa came running outside. "Is she ok? Fleta?" He sat on the ground in the dirt next to her. She was weeping and he was holding her in his arms. "It's ok. I am always going to be here." And he always was.

HOTEL MOTEL

After the incident with the Robert Redford look alike, my Mother began to call my Father again. They decided they were in love again and suddenly we found ourselves in a hotel...a Motel 6 or something like it...Daddy had come to California to get us. We lived in Richmond. Not a rough neighborhood at the time, but plenty of people like us. My grandparents had taken us in and made it fun. They were getting us skating lessons, making sure we ate, and we began to grow...like plants watered with plenty of foundation.

We had cool clothes and some formation of a schedule. I was able to hang out with friends and I was able to sleep. My Dad kept calling. My Mom was dating men who were nice. Men who seemed to fall all over her and even wanted to marry her with her kids. I remember one guy, tall with glasses, who owned a beautiful ranch. We went to visit him, and he was telling my Mom that all of it would be hers. She just had to get a divorce and she and her children would be

Hotel Motel

well taken care of. For some reason, I liked him, and I knew he sincerely loved Mom.

But Dad kept calling. He called her and said he had changed. He would tell her that he had changed. He would tell her many things and she would, unfortunately believe him. The day he showed up to pick us up from my Grandmother's was a horrible day. I was crying. I didn't want to go back into that tornado. He was arguing with my Grandfather, and my Grandmother was crying and pleading with my Mother not to take us away. My Grandfather was holding her back and we were all crying. My Dad told my Mom he had a place for us to stay and that he was going to make a difference in California.

My Mother had lied to my Grandmother the day we left. She had told her that we were headed back to Colorado. That we had a place to live in Denver and that my Father had a good job. She had lied.

We WERE at some cheesy motel in San Francisco near a beach. It actually said Motel on the front and nothing else. It was gray, with white doors that led to the front of the street, which was busy with characters. Prostitutes, drug dealers and the homeless were amongst the stars on the blocks. There was one redhead prostitute who would come and talk to me when I sat on the ground in front of the door. "Hey pretty girl!" I looked up and smiled, "Hey." "What's your name?" "Yvonne." She looked down at me, "That's a pretty name. You know there are no prostitutes named Yvonne. You know why"? I looked up at her and shook my head no. "Because God does not allow girls with pretty names to be hoes. That's what I am. You better not ever let me see you out here either. You hear me?" I nodded yes. "Can you read?" "Yes ma'am." She took a drag of her cigarette, "Good."

"Can you do math?" "Yes ma'am." "Good! You are smart, mannerable and pretty. You can do a lot in life with that. Do you know God? I nodded. "Ok, so good...now if you pray and keep him happy then he won't forsake you like He did me. Lord knows I have been forsaken...over and over again. I don't think God likes me very much." I looked up at her and innocently stated "God likes hoes. He likes everybody and my Grandma told me that God makes Jesus love us whether He likes it or not." She threw her cigarette on the ground. "Ohhh...I didn't know that." She pulled up her skirt. "Well I gotta get back to work...do you know how to write?" "Yes Maam." Ok then...Imma get you some paper so you can write stuff." "Stuff like what?" "I dunno...just stuff you think about." "Oh, like how my Dad beats up my Mom?" She didn't even flinch. "Yes, that too, beautiful little girl".

 She ran across the busy street in high red heels and a leopard skirt. She put her thumb up and soon a car stopped. I saw her jump in the car. I went back in the room. My Brother and Sister were still sleeping. I didn't know where my parents were. They had left this morning and told me to watch my Brother and Sister. They had brought donuts and apples to the room and told me to feed them to my siblings if they wanted to eat. I went to the TV and turned it on. An old Gunsmoke rerun was on. I liked Gunsmoke…it reminded me of my Great Grandma. She used to have a crush on Little Joe and so did I.

SO IT IS THAT I AM

Today I was watching T.D. Jakes and he asked the audience if they thought they were acting like their predators. I raised my eyebrows. "Wow!" He went on to say that we act like our predators because that is where we are stuck. I said to myself yes and yes. It was what had reminded me of the story of Lil Michael.

T.D. Jakes had hit me powerfully with that statement. Then I began to ask...so what do I do to change? Hmmmm he was right when he said, "Be not conformed to this world...be ye transformed." I had done that before I had my children...went to counseling so I would not hurt them; but now it was time to go to the next level. I was going to get aggressive with my story and tell it without reservation.

My Nanna had always said I had to forgive my Father. She said if you don't forgive him then you will carry his sins with you. I would forgive him later in my life because he confessed how he had treated my Mother. I did not want to carry HIS sins because I had plenty to carry of my own.

I was to find out later my Father's side of things and how harshly he had grown up but that will be in "Daddy's side" of his story.

It says all over the bible that the sins of the father are transferred to the next generation and perhaps generations to come. I believe that I did not really get that the curses were attached to me until I was over 40. I remember consciously praying away that curse and felt something within me fighting to let go of it. It had been attached to me for so long. I was tired of carrying the burden of the curse of the generations. It was too damn heavy. Time to release it.

The bible also says in 2 Corinthians 5:17 "Therefore, if anyone is in Christ, he is a new creation. The old has passed away; behold, the new has come." So, when T.D. Jakes asked **"Have you been pulled back far enough to earn the right to know that you have been positioned to prosper by what you endured?"** I knew that God had wanted me to tell this story when I was a little girl. He had given me the experiences I had in hopes of another Woman, another girl or another sufferer coming forward and saying I was in that too. I was that child having to take care of my Brothers and Sisters. I was that child having to take care of my Mother or my Father. I never got to be a child because I was made to endure to carry the load and still come out sitting in the palm of God.

So, for you, this is the end of this story, but I am typing this chapter first.

First, because I know that I will finish this book so that it is the end of letting myself suffer. It will be the end of my letting myself wallow in what used to be this horrible story of a little girl who changed her life. Who decided to take…finally, the gift God gave her a long time ago and…finally…finally do something with it! It is the end of this particular story for you but for me a beginning of an awareness…a literary breath of fresh air. An oxygen tank of life to enjoy and move to the second half of a life filled with smiles, love and joy.

This is, for you, the end of this saga but for me it is an agreement with my life to have what 'I" want, what "I" enjoy, and what "GOD" kept telling me all those years I could have.

For you, these pages close after the last chapter. For me, a new book opens, with new revelations and new lessons that I can now jump into with both feet, wondering…."Now that I am here, how did I get here? What am I learning and what will God give me to take with me in the future?

For you if you are a survivor, you will celebrate this victory with me. Celebrate the gift of life God kept me here for and to know that with whatever happens in the future... "This one's on me."

Charismatic Violence

EPILOGUE

My Mother died on September 16, 2005 from multiple myeloma. She knew three years before she was going to die and instructed my Father not to have a funeral or a memorial. She didn't want anyone lying about how they cared for her when they really didn't. My Dad honored everything she asked, up to the point of not giving any of her ashes to anyone including family. She wanted us to dump her ashes at Seal Rock in California. She loved it there.

My Brother called me to say "Hey, Dad is not eating. He is wasting away, and he will not listen to any of us but...he will listen to you."

As always I went into action for my family and called my Dad and told him that I "needed him" as I was moving back home to Denver.

I moved back home into the house, my Mother died in and her spirit was all over the house. The girls and my family would frequently see shadows moving and feel something sit next to them on the sofa

I had not had a relationship with my Father before, so he began to actually talk to me...have a conversation.

During one of the conversations, I shared with him the church I was going to called Emmanuel Christian Center and asked my Father to come. I was pleasantly surprised when he said yes. He had never gone to church with us. Ever. It was Pastor Alvin Simpkins who got to my Father. His sermons of redemption and forgiveness drew in my whole family.

Today, my Father is an ordained Deacon at his church called Pilgrim Journey Baptist Church under Reverend Robert Simpson, Jr.

My Father, who was an abuser, now often counsels men, who currently or in the past have abused their wives. My Father who is clean and sings in the choir cries often and constantly apologizes for his behavior. He has asked us so many times to forgive him and we forgive him every time he asks. He attends just about every event he can for his family and gives us all the encouragement and love he can muster.

He has shown us that with the desire, one can seek God and if you so choose, you can change.

Epilogue

His apology and prayers had a release for his children which brought about a focus for all of us to heal ourselves to make sure that we conquered the generational curses and hurts that were passed down. He opened up the blessings of God on us through him to where success has been rained down on his Children, his Grandchildren and now his Great Grandchildren.

You see, my Father was made to dance at gun point at seven years old by police officers in Pueblo, Colorado. It was a racist time and they made him dance until "they" got tired. He had just walked to the corner store to get candy.

He saw his Mother get hit in the head with the butt of a rifle by a white man who called her a "black bitch" when the whole family was picking corn in the cornfield.

He was the little kid who every day for years, would take his lunch at recess and go hide somewhere to eat it because they were poor, and his Mom would place a homemade biscuit or a homemade hamburger in the bag for his lunch. He would hide because whatever it was she would make would create a big grease stain on the bottom of his bag and he didn't want the kids to make fun of him.

He is the same man whose Father hit him in the head with a cast iron pan and then let him lay out in the sun for hours while ants and bugs crawled on him and told his Brothers and Sisters, "If you help him I'll kill you."

This is a man who tells me now, "I couldn't do things for you." And then cries, "I didn't have the money to send you to Brown or to Howard".

This is the man who now sees all that my Mother did for him and how much she actually loved him and how... somehow, they managed to stay married for 42 years up until the day she died.

He has come up from the ashes and asked God to help him to be the best Man for my Stepmother Mildean and the best Father, Uncle, Brother example that he can be.

My Mother, well she came into the world a sickly child and throughout her life she consistently suffered pain. She was the female version of Jabez.

The day she died, everyone went outside, and I was left alone with her in the living room. I thought I heard her exhale. I was to dress her and prepare her body to go for cremation. There was a lavender shirt and a deep purple skirt that I bought her, and I knew she loved it. She had told

Epilogue

me about all the compliments she had received when she wore it.

I pulled that, a depends, and clean underwear. Her eyes looked like they were almost closed but not all the way. It seemed like she was still there looking at me. She looked beautiful, not in pain...still.

I began talking to her. "Hi Mommy, I am just going to clean you up ok?" (I had been here before, I had cleaned her up so many times before) I was taking off the old robe, underwear and bra. Removing the wet diaper. I wiped her down so she would not smell. "I am putting on fresh things for you. I remember you used to say that if you were where someone had to transport you, it would be important for your underwear to be beautiful..well,.. sexy."

I giggled to myself. "I am putting on this purple outfit that you like and your little short boots. You are going to look nice." This time when I moved her she was stiff. Her body like a board as I pulled the skirt up to her waist. "Ok, we are ready." I touched her hand and looked at her face, quiet, at peace and her beautiful eyes were still light brown. I knew it was the last time I would see her face. I kissed her on the cheek and whispered, "I love you Mommy".

Charismatic Violence

ABOUT THE AUTHOR

Yvonne York Swain is a graduate of the University of Denver. A native Coloradoan, Yvonne blames her writing interest on her amazing teachers at Denver South High School where her teachers encouraged her to continue to pursue her love of poetry. Exposed to the works of Maya

Angelou, Terry McMillan and Alice Walker Mrs. Swain claims that she walked into the library and asked for books written by Women of Color.

Mrs. Swain is currently married to retired Army Staff Sergeant Clarence Swain who encouraged her to complete her book by saying, "I will read it when you are done." He referred by her as "My Hero". Mrs. Swain states that he not only protected her but honored her vision of completing this book.

Yvonne was born in Pueblo, Colorado in 1964. She was the result of what family deemed as "an accidental" pregnancy and her parents were forced to marry even though they really didn't know each other. In her lifetime, Yvonne has survived abandonment, kidnapping, physical abuse, sexual abuse and codependency. This is the reason Yvonne was asked often by her Daughters to speak to their friends who were living in abusive homes.

Knowing firsthand the child's side of observing abuse, Yvonne has been a leader/counselor for children in various capacities throughout her movement in the U.S.

Epilogue

A proud member of Zeta Phi Beta Sorority Incorporated, Yvonne now lives in Texas and enjoys time with her Husband, three Daughters and their respective families.

1) Marla Gibbs
2) Lucille Ball
3) Lawanda Paige
4) Ja'net DuBois
5)
6) Adele Givens
7) Melanie Camacho
8) Lunelle
9) Aida Rodriquez
10)